THE VINTAGE WAY

CREATING A SCANDINAVIAN-STYLE HOME
WITH PRELOVED FINDS

WRITTEN AND PHOTOGRAPHED BY

Sarah Marie Winther

MITCHELL BEAZLEY

Contents

Introduction

If there's one person who's inspired my chosen interiors style, it's my grandmother. That's not because she's a vintage enthusiast herself, but because she's always prioritized craftsmanship and quality. She was so forward-thinking that nearly all her and my grandfather's mid-century modern furniture from the 1960s still holds up perfectly today. When she moved from her large house to a small apartment a few years ago, she needed to sell the pieces that wouldn't fit in. I took on the task and soon discovered that everything resold really easily, even fetching good prices. This reinforced my belief that, although preowned pieces of designer furniture can be pricey, they are almost always an investment. If you take proper care of them, you are likely to get your money back should you ever choose to sell them.

My grandmother has not only influenced how I feel about quality, but also directly influenced the design of my home. Many of my ornaments belonged to her. For me, these heirlooms (that is, the ones you truly want in your home) are the best form of reuse. Every candlestick, bowl and sculpture remind me of her. While I'm not particularly fond of displaying family photos, I have a deep appreciation of decorative objects that have been passed down to me by loved ones. Each has its own story, much like my vintage finds.

While working on this book, it was important for me to demonstrate that preloved and vintage are not a trend or a fleeting fad destined to fade within a few months or years, and that there is no such thing as a 'vintage style'. Instead, it's a mindset, one that can be embraced no matter your personal taste, the size of your home, your budget or how your preferences evolve over time. With this in mind, I've made a conscious effort to include homes that are vastly different from one another. Later in the book, you'll find everything from small two-room apartments to large villas spanning hundreds of square metres. In some of the homes I've selected, second-hand forms their foundation and is a natural and integral part of the decor. In others, it's the finishing touch that adds personality and character to the space. In the same way, the homeowners have different reasons for choosing second-hand; some dedicate countless hours to hunting down the perfect pieces from specific periods, complete with the right patina, while others are more spontaneous, picking up whatever catches their eye at flea markets or vintage fairs. What unites them, however, is their ability to blend the new with the old, the experimental with the classic, the patinated with the polished, creating spaces that feel both stylish and full of life.

I started writing this book wanting to show people how fulfilling it can be to live with vintage. Not long before, I'd overheard a young woman say she wouldn't buy second-hand furniture because she didn't want to 'live like her grandmother'. I felt an overwhelming urge to prove to her that she didn't have to. So many incredible tables, chairs, bookshelves, lamps, mirrors, vases, candlesticks, ceramics, baskets and art pieces have been produced over the past five decades that she would be able to create a home more beautiful than she could imagine by choosing vintage. Ironically, my own home now resembles my grandmother's more than I ever expected – though I like to think that few grandmothers live quite as stylishly as mine.

Kasannessen
The Ceramist

Poul Kjærholm

Richard Manz

Christian Holmsted Olesen

's

ARNE JACOBSEN

AXEL SALTO – PÅ PAPIR

BJØRN NØRGAARD
ELMGREEN & DRAGSET RE-MODELLING THE WORLD

Dan Flavin Drawing

LARS NORELL — ERIK THOMMESEN

MESTERVÆRKER

Koppel

Elisabeth Frenkema

LUNDSTRØM

DANSK ARKITEKTU

PART ONE

✕

The Vintage Way

Why buy vintage?

If someone were to ask me that question, I'd be tempted to answer, 'Why not?' But I'm aware that not everyone is as keen on second-hand items as I am, which is why I'll explore here the many advantages of buying something that has been in someone else's hands before being in yours.

✕ You're doing the planet a tremendous favour

by purchasing something that's already been produced rather than contributing to increased consumption and rising CO_2 emissions by taking home something brand-new. Every single day, thousands upon thousands of products are made, and many of them end up languishing in drawers, cupboards, lofts, cellars and garages, only to be sold eventually at a car boot sale (garage sale) or, worse, disposed of as bulky waste. Whenever I visit a flea market or a charity shop, I see shelves overflowing with goods, some that haven't even been removed from their packaging. It's such a shame that all these precious resources have gone into making something that is never ever put to use. By buying something others have bought before you – whether in the 1950s or a decade ago – you're taking a stand against throwaway culture.

✕ You get objects that last longer

because the vast majority of furniture from the past is of better quality than what's available today. This is largely due to the fact that joiners and cabinetmakers then used more solid (and therefore more expensive) materials, many pieces were handmade, and the standard for newly produced items was higher. One of the things I love most about buying furniture and accessories with decades of history is the genuine craftsmanship that often lies behind them. Fifty or so years ago, the strategy of planned obsolescence wasn't nearly as widespread as it is today. Items weren't designed with a built-in limited lifespan to drive sales. On the contrary, they had to be as durable as possible, and people often took better care of their belongings because they couldn't afford to replace them so easily. Therefore, you often get much better value for money on the second-hand market – for example, glass instead of plastic, leather instead of polyurethane, and solid wood instead of veneer.

✕ You save money in the long term

because used furniture is generally cheaper than new. At the same time, they often hold their value. The moment you push a shopping cart full of goods through the checkout at a modern home store, they lose value, and you'll never be able to sell them for what you paid. Conversely, if you find a bargain and take good care of it, you will almost always be able to sell it again for at least the same price. If it's designer furniture, it could even become an investment for the future. Even though I have no intention of parting with my belongings, it gives me peace of mind that my dining table and chairs could help me put food on the table (or kitchen counter) if I were to suddenly lose my job or face unexpected expenses.

✕ You end up with a more personal and individual home

that doesn't look like your neighbour's or something in a catalogue. This is perhaps the most important reason I buy vintage. There's simply nothing more satisfying than when guests compliment my home and ask where I bought a particular piece, and I can say, 'I found it at a car boot sale for £5' or, 'It's a 1960s original I found online.' It's fun to own something unique, and it's good to know my friends or colleagues can't just go on a quick shopping trip and buy the same thing. Not everything in my home is vintage or even preowned, but visitors always notice the pieces that are and find them the most interesting.

How to navigate the world of vintage

I completely understand those who hesitate when it comes to buying anything preowned. When you buy something used, there's no accompanying guarantee, and you have no earthly idea how the piece has been looked after, unless you inspect it in person and talk to the owner, which isn't always feasible.

Fortunately, there are ways to get rid of even the most unpleasant odours from old wooden furniture. Airing it out, wiping it with white vinegar or placing bowls of baking soda or acetic acid inside can help absorb unwanted smells. Along with a thorough sanding and a coat of oil, furniture soap or paint, you can genuinely make a piece of furniture look as good as new (see also page 22). I also cover what to consider when assessing the condition of a preloved item and which (few) things are better purchased new rather than used (see page 16).

Naturally, finding the perfect vintage piece requires more time and effort than walking into a shop or browsing a website for a newly produced alternative. Generally, the rule with second-hand shopping is that the less you want to pay, the more time you need to invest in finding it. I have several friends who feel utterly overwhelmed the moment they enter a flea market and simply cannot face digging through piles of worthless bits and bobs in search of a treasure that may or may not be lurking at the bottom. This reaction is completely valid, and if you feel this way, you're

in luck because there are countless shops and digital platforms that have done the hard work for you. Often, items are presented in beautiful and inspiring settings, making it easy for customers to see their value. In return, you may have to pay a little (or quite a lot more) for them, but if you don't have much time in your daily life, the extra money is likely well spent.

Personally, I love the thrill of hunting for the perfect find. Over the years I've become so discerning that unless I find something I've been seeking for a long time but without success, and it's in absolutely perfect condition, I won't pay the price that a high-end store would demand for it. However, if you lack the patience, energy or desire to embark on such a search, vintage shops are a great place to start – you'll also find a guide to these later in the book (see page 221). I would dare say that once you start taking an interest in sourcing vintage items, you will gradually become better at spotting those truly great finds, even if they are hidden under a thick layer of dust and dirt or surrounded by clutter.

You might also resist buying items with a bit of age to them because

you favour a light, minimalist style and worry that your living room will end up looking like a museum, a flea market or your grandmother's sitting room. Fortunately, there are plenty of ways to incorporate vintage finds seamlessly into your decor so that no one will even notice what is new and what is old. There's no rule to say that your home must consist of 100 per cent second-hand items, or even 50, 25 or 10 per cent. For instance, in a beautifully designed kitchen with a new worktop, cabinets, fixtures, appliances and lights, a couple of old chopping boards or bowls can be the perfect way to break up the sleek, coordinated look. The devil, after all, is in the detail.

What to know before you start buying

Just because you're buying second-hand doesn't mean you can shop recklessly. If you find yourself purchasing furniture or knick-knacks that you neither need nor have space for, you can quickly end up with overcrowded and haphazardly decorated rooms, and your home will start to resemble a flea market.

Before embarking on your search, take stock of what you already have and what you need or would like to replace. Most people have a mix of heirlooms, old IKEA furniture from their first home, newly produced items from department stores and, perhaps, a handful of more expensive designer pieces. Go through one room at a time and jot down your impressions. Does the room feel airy or cluttered? Is the furniture functional and comfortable? What works well together and what doesn't? Is there sufficient seating, storage space and lighting?

Write down in detail what you're looking for. Note the measurements of the room (or rooms) you're going to redesign. If you're physically searching for vintage pieces, keep a tape measure in your bag or pocket to ensure you return home with something that fits the space. If you're browsing online, check the measurements of any pieces first to avoid falling in love with something that's too big or too small. If no sizes are given, ask for them.

Of course, there should also be room for impulse buys if something fantastic presents itself, but generally it's a good idea to ask yourself: 'Does this item fit the aesthetic I'm aiming for? Does it serve a purpose – perhaps a functional one?' I used to buy far too many vintage pieces because I felt it was my calling to rescue them from being hidden away on a distant shelf in a charity shop or, even worse, being thrown away. However, in recent years, I've become better at telling myself that, although I may recognize a piece as beautiful, I don't need to bring it home and it would be far more useful to someone else.

While I advocate buying as much as possible second-hand, there are certain items for which this approach is trickier. Generally, you should be mindful of the condition of furniture intended for daily use, such as dining tables, dining chairs, lounge chairs and sofas, as well as of smaller pieces like china and baskets. These can, and often will in the near future, show signs of wear and tear, so it's important to check their condition or ask the seller if you can't assess it in person. For example, the back of a shell chair may have become soft, while it's possible the cushions or webbing on the bottom of a sofa will soon wear out after many years of faithful service. Therefore, try out any seating piece and check that a dining table is stable and doesn't wobble. If the veneer is damaged or there are loose joints, chips, cracks or other flaws, carefully consider whether you could – and, realistically, would – do the repairs yourself. Alternatively, could they be fixed by a professional, and would it be worth it in relation to the price of the piece?

I have a weakness for old watering cans, and on one occasion bought a beautiful copper one. It was quite tarnished in places, but I didn't think much about that until I got home and discovered that the corrosion had made a hole in the bottom of the can, causing it to leak. I managed to patch the hole with Super glue, but it could be that you don't have the skills or the inclination to make such repairs. Bear in mind that for teapots, plates and the like, repairing interior cracks or chips with glue can even pose health risks. Always check vulnerable areas such as the handle on a basket, the back of a chair or the corners of a table before buying. If an item looks very worn, it's best to pass and wait for a better-maintained example to come along – but if the piece is very special and you

✕

A workspace need not be furnished with a classic desk and office chair. As long as the furniture is comfortable, you can opt for vintage alternatives. Left: An old architect's table is paired with a 1970s chair by Swiss designer Émile Baumann. The magazine holder is from Alessi, while the artwork was found in a second-hand shop. Below, left: An easy way to create a cohesive arrangement is to group items of similar shades and matching surfaces. Below, right: Kitchen interiors often prioritize functionality but, if space allows, paintings and sculptures in harmony with the rest of the home add a refined touch.

have been looking for something like it for a while, try to negotiate the price and come to a compromise.

That said, many second-hand items do show more or less visible signs of aging. If these signs don't affect functionality, they are referred to as 'patina' rather than 'wear'. When it comes to materials like solid wood, natural stone, metals or leather, patina will manifest as unique colour variations and textures. You shouldn't view this as a negative – it can actually increase the value of, say, furniture, as it tells the story of the piece, giving it a character and depth that new furniture lacks. A good example of this is the Spanish chair by Danish designer Børge Mogensen. Many believe that the chair looks entirely wrong when it first leaves the factory: the leather is completely uniform in colour and texture, and the wood is light, as it hasn't yet been 'broken in'. When such a chair acquires its very first scratch or blemish, this stands out distinctly, whereas on a well-used piece, the patina simply adds to the story of the furniture.

Where to look and what to look for

First and foremost, let's agree on what we're talking about here. You've probably come across the terms 'vintage', 'antique' and 'retro' before – and they are often used interchangeably – but they refer to quite different styles and eras.

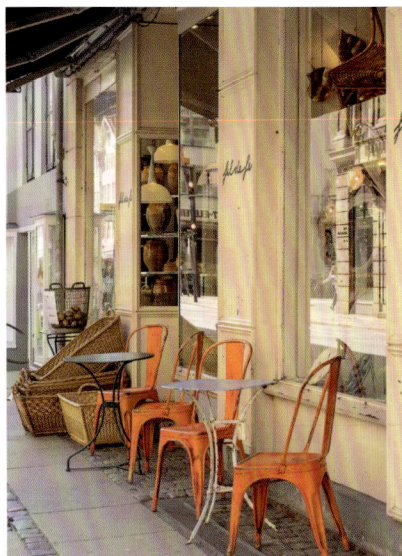

The word 'vintage' originates from the old French for 'grape harvest': *vendange*. Initially, the word was used to describe the year or location in which a wine was produced, and it referred particularly to high-quality wines from a specific harvest. Over time, the meaning of vintage has extended beyond the world of wine to encompass items considered collectable or of high quality, especially those from a previous era. While there is no set age for something to be called vintage, an item is generally considered as such if it is between 20 and 99 years old. This means that IKEA furniture from the 1990s and early 2000s can now be classified as vintage (and it is increasingly being sold at higher prices). However, vintage pieces are typically characterized by their craftmanship and attention to detail and authenticity; a true vintage item shouldn't merely belong to an era – it should epitomize it.

The term 'antique' refers to items that are 100 years old or more. These pieces are valued for their historical significance, rarity and craftsmanship. Antiques can originate from any part of the world,

providing a glimpse into different cultures and periods. They often require careful preservation and can represent a significant investment.

The term 'retro' refers to a style that imitates trends from the 1950s, '60s and '70s, and is often characterized by bold, colourful and eclectic designs. Unlike their vintage or antique counterparts, retro items are not necessarily old and can also be newly produced to replicate the style of a particular era. It's a playful nod to the past, celebrating nostalgia within a modern context.

Now that you're familiar with the meaning of vintage, how do you go about finding and buying those exciting pieces? You may already have an idea of the look you're after but are unsure of what to ask for. Browsing in person is straightforward because you naturally gravitate towards what you like. However, online shopping presents endless options, countless websites and inconsistent labelling, making it essential that you know what to type into the search bar at the outset. On the opposite page, you'll find some useful search terms to kick-start your vintage hunt but keep in mind that these suggestions are meant only as inspiration and are far from exhaustive. Fortunately, most platforms use sophisticated algorithms that quickly learn your preferences and will suggest similar vintage items.

I recommend exploring auction sites that will ship to your country. For example, if you're based in Europe, as I am, Bukowskis, Auctionet and Catawiki are reliable options, offering a wide selection of vintage pieces. It's also worth looking at eBay, Etsy and other vintage-specific marketplaces.

✕ Designer searches

Searching for producers and manufacturers of furniture will broaden your selection and help you discover lesser-known designers whose work is often more affordable than that of the major names. For instance, instead of searching for the mid-century French designer and architect Charlotte Perriand, you could search for Cassina, the Italian manufacturer behind many of the remarkable pieces of furniture from this period.

✕ Era searches

It is always a good idea to search for design periods and styles, as well as materials (see right). There are many fantastic pieces of furniture to be found out there, together with lamps and artworks, without well-known names (and expensive price tags) attached to them.

✕ Material searches

Many high-quality furniture items are defined by their materials rather than by a specific designer. Searching for 'brass details', for example, could unearth well-priced, timeless pieces that might otherwise pass unnoticed.

American
· Norman Cherner
· Ray & Charles Eames
· Paul McCobb
· George Nelson
· Isamu Noguchi

Danish
· Nanna Ditzel
· Arne Jacobsen
· Finn Juhl
· Poul Kjærholm
· Poul Henningsen
· Børge Mogensen
· Verner Panton
· Hans J Wegner

Finnish
· Alvar Aalto
· Eero Saarinen
· Ilmari Tapiovaara
· Paavo Tynell
· Tapio Wirkkala

French
· Pierre Chapo
· Michel Ducaroy
· Pierre Paulin
· Charlotte Perriand
· Jean Prouvé

Italian
· Achille & Pier
· Franco Albini
· Mario Bellini
· Giacomo Castiglioni
· Vico Magistretti
· Gino Sarfatti

Swedish
· Gunnar Asplund
· Hans-Agne Jakobsson
· Arne Norell
· Bruno Mathsson
· Roland Wilhelmsson

Bauhaus (1919–1933)
Key features: Clean geometric shapes, minimalist aesthetics, functionality over decoration, industrial materials like steel and glass.

Art Deco (1920s–1930s)
Key features: Bold geometric patterns, streamlined forms, luxurious materials like chrome, glass, lacquer and exotic woods.

Mid-Century Modern (1940s–1960s)
Key features: Clean lines, organic shapes, functionality, use of innovative materials like moulded plywood, fibreglass and plastic.

Space Age (1950s–1970s)
Key features: Futuristic shapes, bold colours such as orange, white and metallic tones, innovative materials like plastic and fibreglass.

Brutalism (1950s–1970s)
Key features: Massive, block-like forms, chunky, geometric shapes, and materials like concrete, steel and pine wood with a raw, unrefined aesthetic.

· Ash
· Birch
· Burlwood
· Elm
· Oak
· Oregon pine / pine
· Rattan
· Rosewood
· Teak
· Walnut

· Aluminium
· Brass
· Bronze
· Chrome
· Steel

· Granite
· Marble
· Slate

· Acrylic
· Bakerlite
· Fibreglass

Finding hidden gems online

✄

Social media platforms have made it easier than ever to discover unique vintage pieces from sellers near and far. Facebook Marketplace, for example, is an excellent resource for affordable furniture and decor, but the sheer volume of listings can lead to your overlooking a true gem. The following tips should help you navigate this marketplace effectively and secure the best deals.

Train the algorithm
to show you what you want. If you're looking for a vintage Italian floor lamp, say, begin simply by searching for 'vintage Italian floor lamp' a few times a day and saving items that interest you, even if you don't plan to buy them. Saving listings helps the algorithm to learn your preferences and prioritize newly listed items that match your taste, giving you the chance to spot the best deals early and message the seller before anyone else.

Verify pricing
on other websites when you spot something intriguing to ensure you're not overpaying and to help verify the authenticity of the item. A good rule of thumb is that a price is fair if it's more than 50 per cent lower than the price that similar items sell for on high-end platforms like 1stDibs and Chairish.

Act quickly
when you find something you like. Items tend to sell fast on Facebook Marketplace, especially since communication via Messenger is instant. Try not to hesitate if you fall in love with an item. If you're on the hunt for something specific, consider setting up notifications to alert you when similar items become available.

✄

Instagram is another platform that expands your options, with its focus on high-quality visuals, making it easier to connect with potential sellers – but it also requires patience and quick thinking. Highly coveted items are often snapped up within minutes of hitting the feed. Here's what you need to know in order to get started.

Follow hashtags
Hashtags are crucial on Instagram, as they help you discover new posts from people that you don't already follow and allow you to search for specific names, eras and materials. While broader tags like #vintagedecor, #vintagefurniture and #midcenturymodern are useful, don't hesitate to explore niche options! If you're looking for, let's say, a 1960s Murano floor lamp by Carlo Nason for Mazzega, consider searching for #murano, #muranoglass, #carlonason, #nasonlamp and #mazzega. It's also wise to check what hashtags your favourite sellers use in their posts, and follow those that catch your interest.

Make sure to investigate
the reputation and legitimacy of each seller, particularly if you're in the market for more valuable designer items. Look for a complete, professional profile with a clear profile picture, a well-written bio and consistent posts. Genuine and trustworthy sellers typically have a history of posting their products and engaging with their audience through comments and likes. Also, keep in mind that having fewer followers doesn't necessarily indicate poorer quality; some store owners might just not be very internet savvy or may conduct most of their business in a physical shop. Ultimately, you want to find accounts that align with your personal taste.

Review story highlights
to see how a seller might be tracking what's still unclaimed. Sellers will often compile available items in their highlights or use custom hashtags you can follow. If they have an Instagram shop set up, click their 'view shop' button to browse available listings.

Read the captions carefully
Captions provide essential details about an item, including history, measurements, price, how to buy, description and/or history and, importantly, disclosure of any defects or issues. Most of your questions will often be answered right there, but if not, you can always message the seller via DM for clarification.

Be aware of shipping costs
You could end up paying as much for shipping as for the item itself, especially if the seller is overseas. This can significantly impact the overall value of your purchase and may influence your decision to buy.

Buying on trading platforms is very different from buying on auction sites and they require quite distinct strategies. Below are some useful tips for navigating the auction world, which to some can appear intimidating and competitive.

Read descriptions carefully
Check dimensions and examine the images closely. There's no return policy when buying at auction, so be certain that the measurements suit your needs and that the condition of the item is satisfactory. If you're buying lamps or other electronics with plugs on an international auction site, check whether the plugs will work with your outlets. If not, consider whether you could replace the plugs yourself.

Hold off before placing your bid
If five people are bidding on an item and you jump in early, you'll likely drive the price up far more than if you wait patiently until three or four bidders have dropped out. This approach is called bidder exhaustion and is a highly effective strategy.

Be careful not to forget the item entirely – make a note of when the auction ends and set a timer on your phone.

Raise the stakes
A few minutes before the auction closes, enter the fray with your maximum bid straightaway, so that any bidders hoping to top you are immediately met with a counterbid. This move often deters others before they reach your maximum. They will be thinking, 'All right, this bidder really intends to win.' Confidence is a key part of bidding strategy.

Think ahead when plotting your strategy for bidding
It's no surprise that shipping costs for antique and vintage furniture can turn a total steal into a huge money pit – most auction sites calculate a minimum price for shipping, which is typically stated below the leading bid, but otherwise you can use a site like uShip. With this site, you essentially key in what you're shipping and from where to where, what the measurements are and the approximate weight. You're then given an estimate of what you should be paying. If you're flexible on timing, you can even name your own price. Transportation is GPS-tracked, you can add insurance, and the service operates worldwide.

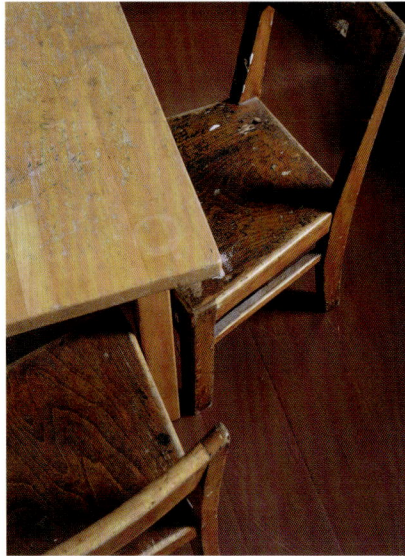

Bringing furniture back to life

It is rare for a vendor at a flea market or the staff at a charity shop to take the time to do any restoration work before putting their furniture up for sale. However, with a few simple techniques, you can refresh and revive these pieces yourself.

Unless you already know how to upholster, I'd always recommend leaving that part of the restoration process to the professionals, but anyone can freshen up wooden furniture. With care, you can give a worn, scratched, stained or poorly painted piece an entirely new look. It's easier if the piece is untreated, soap-treated or oiled, rather than lacquered, but with enough effort, it is possible to remove the lacquer too.

Start by giving the piece a proper clean. Furniture quickly collects dirt, dust and grime, which should be removed with warm water and furniture soap. Stiff brushes and washing-up sponges can easily cause damage, so use a soft cloth instead. Make sure you reach into all the crevices. If the piece has been treated previously, it's a good idea to use wood cleaner after the water treatment to remove any oil and soap residues.

You will probably want to remove any layers of old paint, which tends to chip over time, and if you want to repaint the piece a new colour, the end result will look significantly better if the old paint is removed first. An effective method is to coat the wood in brown soap and cover it with cling film (plastic wrap). The soap will slowly but surely soften the paint and then loosen it. Let the mixture sit for a few days, then remove it with a scraper. Brown soap works more slowly than the harsher chemical paint removers on the market but is gentler on the environment. Afterwards, wash the wood with water and acetic acid (2 litres/4 pints of water to $\frac{1}{4}$ litre/$\frac{1}{2}$ pint of acetic acid) to neutralize the process. Allow the wood to dry before proceeding.

Once the furniture is cleaned and, if necessary, stripped of paint, it's time for the hard and messy work: sanding. Always use fine, high-quality sandpaper to prevent any damage, and make sure you work in the same direction as the wood grain to avoid leaving any marks. A sander can take the place of elbow grease, except, to be on the safe side, in any nooks, carvings and corners. When you've finished, wipe the piece well with a damp cloth to avoid having sanding dust between the furniture and the paint or other finishing. Let the wood dry completely before continuing.

So, what treatment should your piece have? In the 1990s, it was very popular in Scandinavia to soap-treat wooden furniture to give it an almost white finish. Nowadays, though, many prefer to highlight the wood's natural glow and grain patterns, often opting for an oil treatment instead. This also makes the wood more durable, as the oil hardens on the surface. I would always recommend this approach.

⤬

Opposite: Some pieces of vintage furniture can be used as they are, while others need a little care to look their best, be functional or suit your home's interior style. Left: In a light-toned setting, pine works well – either in its natural hue, treated with furniture soap, or finished with white oil. Many people avoid lacquered pine because it tends to develop a strong yellow tone over time, but the lacquer can often be sanded off quite easily. Remember to switch from coarse to fine sandpaper as soon as the lacquer is removed, to avoid scratching the soft, raw surface.

For larger surfaces, such as tabletops, cabinet doors or drawers, a paint roller can be useful – it's quick, is easy to use and provides a smooth, even finish. However, a completely smooth surface can seem out of place on a vintage piece, so I would usually recommend painting with a brush, as the brush strokes give a subtle, more authentic look with visible texture. A brush is also necessary for smaller items of furniture and pieces with detailing. When painting, work quickly and systematically, starting with one area and moving to the next before the paint dries. Always use long, soft strokes and avoid overly thick layers. In this way, you'll achieve an even surface without visible overlaps or streaks.

Just remember that oil on an exposed surface, such as a dining tabletop, will wear down over time, so it's important to maintain the treatment.

You can also, of course, paint your furniture. Paint can completely transform a piece and is a good option if, for example, the natural colour of the wood doesn't suit your home or if it's heavily worn. After cleaning and sanding, use primer to help the paint adhere better and be evenly distributed on the surface. If your furniture is entirely untreated, you can use a regular primer, whereas an adhesion primer is needed if the furniture is lacquered or already painted. Remember to check the tin for the recommended waiting time before painting over it.

When choosing paint, consider how the furniture will be used. For a frequently used piece, like a chair, durability is key. Opt for a paint that can withstand wiping without easily wearing off, and avoid overly thin formulas that may run and make it harder to achieve a smooth, even finish. Decorative items will probably be fine with a less durable paint.

PART TWO

✕

The
Homes

Layers of Time

I'm not entirely sure if I'm the person in this book with the largest proportion of vintage as opposed to new in their home, but I'm definitely among the finalists. I don't know when it happened, but at some point in my life, I subconsciously decided that second-hand was better than new. Since then, I've delved into different design eras, movements, materials and production methods. The furniture in my home is therefore a reflection of my deep interest in design and how it has developed over the last 50 years.

For example, the Rag chair by Danish designer Bernt Petersen was one of the first pieces I acquired when my partner and I moved from a 43-square-metre (463-square-foot) apartment to our current 95-square-metre (1,022-square-foot) apartment. I knew that this easy chair would offer incredible comfort with its high back and neck support, but it was just as much the simple design language that appealed to me. In addition, when the chair was first sold in 1965, it was at a much more affordable price than similar architect-designed lounge

Opposite: The apartment's interior is defined by light surfaces and furniture made from natural materials. Above left: In the living room, the narrow cabinet is a prototype purchased from a local carpenter, while the small stool was found on Facebook Marketplace. Above right: One corner of the room is dedicated to a collection of vinyl records, stacked on an Oregon pine shelving unit, also from Marketplace. The Gridmo seating module, designed by Peter J Lassen for Montana in the 1990s, was bought on Instagram, as was the painting, while the drawing and lithograph were found at flea markets.

✕

Previous pages: In the light-filled living room, the blue-bordered Swedish rug was a true steal at a Copenhagen flea market, while the grey-painted bench came from a gymnasium. The Mogens Andersen lithograph was bought at auction; Isamu Noguchi designed the ceiling lamp for Vitra. Right: The dining room is simply furnished with a solid pine table and fibreglass DSR chairs by Charles and Ray Eames, from the 1950s. I found the table for a good price on a local sales platform. It doesn't have a label, but I've since discovered it was likely made by Roland Wilhelmsson. The ceiling lamp is an original Radiohus pendant by Vilhelm Lauritzen; the pictures are lithographic exhibition posters by Mogens Andersen, Axel Salto and Emma Kohlmann. Below: The pared-back entrance hall is an indicator of the calm interior to come. Opposite: Pine and patinated brass are recurring materials in the details of furniture and accessories. The bowl and candleholder were found at flea markets; a local glass blower made the vase. Designed by Karin Mobring for IKEA in 1970, the chair in chrome and patinated aniline leather then cost less than £18 ($23).

chairs available at the time. In this way, Petersen helped democratize Danish design by making it accessible to a wider audience. The same can be said of Ingvar Kamprad, founder of IKEA. Although the company's furniture portfolio today bears more of the hallmarks of mass production and functionality, in the 1960s and '70s, it had some truly spectacular designs, which hold their appeal today, such as the Amiral chair by Karin Mobring, a standout piece in my collection. I love the combination of cognac saddle leather and chrome – a beautiful contrast to the many wooden pieces in my living room.

When it comes to the smaller details, my style is defined by a dualism: a love for unique pieces with an interesting story and a genuine desire to live with clean surfaces and open, uncluttered spaces. It's a balance that's constantly challenged, as I'm daily tempted by something else catching my eye, but over the years, I've fine-tuned my ability to assess whether an item will fit the available space and suit my evolving style. It helps that I'm nowhere near sentimental – if I sense I've accumulated too much in a period, I'm quick to sort things out again to restore harmony.

When we took over this apartment, it had been in the hands of the same owner for 60 years. The rooms had been left largely untouched, with varnished wooden floors, stucco ceilings and a drying line in the bedroom. Since then, we've renovated the space but with a respect – almost a reverence – for what we inherited. In Copenhagen, original apartments of this size are rare, as most have been renovated multiple times. This one had only a tiny loo (toilet) and no sink, so we needed to install a new bathroom before moving in. The kitchen, though functional, was 56 years old and of inferior quality, so after two years of consideration, we decided to invest in a new one that would make better use of the relatively large space. Those two years not only served as a lead-up to making the investment, but also made us clear in our minds what we actually wanted, allowing us to look beyond trends and choose a classic, high-quality kitchen that would be timeless. It was crucial that both the new bathroom and kitchen – rooms that often stand out stylistically in a classic 19th-century home – reflected the architecture and superior craftsmanship of the period in which the building was constructed.

⤬

Below and opposite: When we took over the apartment, the original pine floors were lacquered and completely orange, so we sanded them ourselves and treated them with natural soap. We then replaced the old kitchen with a new one from Funkiskök, which suits the age and style of the building. The chopping boards, spice jars and storage containers were all bought second-hand. Opal glass lamps by Vilhelm Lauritzen (now produced by Louis Poulsen) hang over the kitchen counter. The lithograph is by Mogens Andersen, the kettle by Alessi, and the 1960s teapot by Michael Breum.

✕

Above: The bedroom is intentionally furnished more sparsely than the rest of the apartment, creating a calm atmosphere that invites restful sleep. Opposite: The brass display case in the bedroom is an heirloom from my grandmother, as is the shelving unit with fabric boxes, used for storing clothes. In the office, set up in the former maid's room, the white-painted wooden desk was discovered in a skip (dumpster). I acquired the wicker office chair on Instagram. The artwork in the black frame is an original exhibition catalogue by Hans Arp, which was a gift; I found the old newspaper advertisement and framed it.

If you look around my home, you'll find hardly any new pieces. It's been years since I last stepped into a furniture store and, aside from pans, knives and other kitchen essentials that naturally wear down with use, I have little interest in acquiring anything new. I simply place greater value on preowned pieces, and if I do eventually buy something like a lamp new, it's only after months of unsuccessful searching for a similar one second-hand. Since I own many items from different eras, I've focused on creating a calm and cohesive look through the colours in each room. The walls, furniture and textiles are

in neutral tones and light wood, so that the art and artefacts can speak a bit louder. Strong colours have never been my style – I'm far more interested in texture, tactility and sensuousness, and I use my hands as much as my eyes when shopping. I don't much care for smooth, uniform surfaces and prefer to surround myself with natural materials like linen, leather, stoneware, natural stone and wood. In fact, the only plastic items I have at home are my bedside lamps. Designed by Sergio Brazzoli for Harvey Guzzini in the 1970s, they have scratches and scuffs, just the way I like it.

The Old Laundry

In many large cities around the world, old industrial buildings that no longer serve a purpose are being converted into modern, attractive homes, complete with high ceilings, large windows and a raw charm you wouldn't find in a typical apartment. Transformations like this are often led by investors, but if you're daring, creative and practical, you could take on such a project yourself. That's exactly what Esben Cordius did when he set his sights on an old laundry just a few hundred metres (yards) from his then-apartment. The premises had been vacant for a long time, and he immediately saw their potential. 'I was actually beaten to it by some property speculators, who wanted to convert the laundry into a regular apartment, but I managed to convince them to sell it to me instead,' Esben explains.

Then came the administrative work of applying for building permits, followed by ten months of intense renovation before the apartment was ready for Esben to move in to. Apart from the electrical and plumbing work, he did everything himself with help from his father, who works as a carpenter. From the beginning, Esben's vision was of an apartment with an open-plan layout and the minimum of doors and corridors. The large room facing the street would serve as the kitchen, dining and living area, and the rear room facing the courtyard would be the bedroom. The end result is an airy and open living space, with an abundance of natural light. Esben, with a background in furniture and textile sales, has decorated the apartment with a stylish mix of modern design and interesting vintage finds.

Right: Like so much in the apartment, Esben's collection of kitchenware is almost entirely second-hand. The blue glass jar was designed by Danish artist Per Lütken for Holmegaard Glasværk. Opposite and overleaf: The renovation has given the apartment an open and fluid feel. A mix of classic chairs by Arne Jacobsen, Børge Mogensen and Bruno Rey surround the dining table in a design by Poul Kjærholm. The lamp over the table is Vilhelm Lauritzen's Radiohus pendant, now produced by Louis Poulsen.

Dansk møbelkunst i det 20. århundred

Dansk møbelkunst i det 20. århundred

Olafur Eliasson
Rummets bevægelse

Om at opleve design

Thomas
Dickson

JEAN PROUVÉ

GISELE

FINN JUHL   LIV VÆRK VERD

S T A R C

Herman Miller
A Way of Living

JOACHIM WELLER

※

Above: Thanks to the slanted matte glass panels, the large windows facing the street let in plenty of light while still ensuring privacy. An open shelving unit separates the kitchen and dining areas within the expansive space. Opposite: The minimalist brushed steel kitchen is a perfect match for the apartment's previous life as a laundry. The pendant lamps above the worktop were designed by Achille & Pier Giacomo Castiglioni for Flos in the 1990s. Overleaf: The living room is furnished with the Arbour sofa and Crate chair, both from HAY, together with the Cappellini Knotted Chair by Marcel Wanders. An old organ pipe from a church acts as a sculpture by the window.

Esben's passion for vintage gems started when he was 16. Living in the countryside, his family had a neighbour who had spent 20 years clearing out estates, accumulating a vast collection of items in his large farm barn rather than selling them. However, Esben remembers that one year the neighbour set up a flea market, and he went in and bought a few items, which he then got his mum to collect for him. 'That's when the fascination began, and I actually ended up buying quite a few things from him, which I then sold on. It evolved into my father and I driving around in his van, buying items, refurbishing them and then selling them. At one point, we even got a storage unit. We really enjoyed it, and we kept the best things for ourselves. Some people go fishing together – we went to flea markets,' Esben says, adding that he has just finished refurbishing the basement that came with the laundry, where he has built a large workshop. With this new space, he is finally able to start buying and selling again. Most of his bargain hunting takes place at flea markets, for which he always gets up early to be ready and waiting when they open. This approach has led to many excellent finds over the years.

'Now and then, I end up buying something that doesn't quite fit in with my style or for which I can't find a good place in my home. On several occasions, I've been fortunate enough to swap the piece for something I'm actually looking for,' he notes.

In the old floor plans for the building from 1934, you can see that it initially housed a grocery store and a colonial goods store, before being converted into a laundry in 1986. Thanks to the extensive refurbishment and beautiful decor, it's hard to place the apartment in a

particular time period, but here and there, traces of its former self as a laundry can still be found. In the living room, Esben has kept the heavy wood and glass street door; in the bathroom, you step onto a rustic concrete floor and a worn but beautiful terrazzo floor in the shower.

Originally, the entire floor of the apartment was terrazzo, but there were too many holes in it and uneven areas, not to mention that it was far too cold – there was no underfloor heating or downstairs neighbour to warm it up. So, he decided to have

Above and opposite: Esben's home is, in every sense, a personal retreat, with the bright bedroom seamlessly connected to the living and kitchen areas. A stainless-steel Triangolo chair, designed by Per Holland Bastrup in 1989 and now produced by Frama, sits alongside the bed on a HAY frame. Esben is drawn to Japanese culture and aesthetics, and has travelled extensively in the country. On one trip, he brought back the decorative paper dragonfly seen on the wall above the vintage wooden chair. The small artwork on the shelf above the dragonfly is a lithograph by Emma Kohlmann.

the floor levelled and to lay down wide Dinesen Douglas fir boards. In the bathroom, he plans to install a new linoleum floor, which is warmer underfoot. 'I'm generally not afraid to dive into things, probably because I'm good at finding solutions and I don't mind making compromises,' he says. 'It's not crucial to me that things turn out exactly as I imagined – it will turn out well anyway, and nothing compares to the feeling of having done something yourself.'

What makes this interior so interesting is the mix of innovative and classic designs. Working at HAY, the Danish design brand, gave Esben great insight into the international design world, and it opened his eyes to the possibility of blending Danish design with French, Italian, Swedish and German styles. While he mainly sources his furniture second-hand, he also enjoys discovering new and experimental design during his travels. A couple of years ago, he made a particularly good purchase in Stockholm. While staying in the city for a few days between Christmas and New Year, he noticed that the renowned design store Nordiska Galleriet was holding a clearance sale.

Fortunately, a green Cappellini Knotted Chair by Marcel Wanders was among the discounted items – and he even managed to get a bit of extra discount on top. 'I took it with me on the train from Stockholm. It was in the luggage rack, and I was practically sitting underneath it,' laughs Esben.

When it comes to smaller items, he is particularly fond of ceramics, but he has also recently developed an interest in glass, especially Italian glass such as Murano and Venini. Furthermore, he dreams of finding something Italian from the '70s and '80s, maybe a chair or a lamp, made of plastic. For Esben, the main reason for buying second-hand is that it is difficult to find new products of the same quality as their vintage counterparts. 'Also, it is quite fascinating to me that the designer of a classic piece of furniture was so forward-thinking at the time that someone like me would still want to buy it today. This is evident in how furniture manufacturers continue to relaunch old designs.'

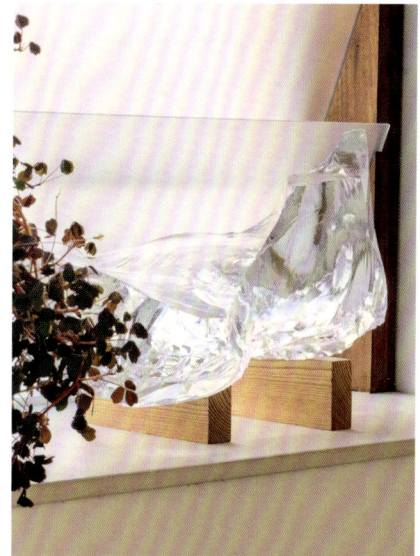

✕TIP

Art is more than just posters and paintings. Esben incorporates all sorts of things in the apartment, from a restored church organ pipe to a large piece of glass from an old factory and a weathered stoneware plate, repurposing them as decorative sculptures and three-dimensional wall art and adding a vibrancy to the decor. You could also introduce elements like woven tapestries or masks to create contrast with more traditional art. These tactile pieces can be displayed on their own or as part of a gallery wall.

✕

Opposite: There are only three doors in the apartment: at the front, at the back leading to the courtyard, and for the bathroom, which Esben has painted a beautiful dusty blue. The stool and the large preserving jar, now used as a plant pot, are second-hand finds, while the floor lamp is a design by Isamu Noguchi for Vitra. The ceramic tile artwork is Esben's own creation.

✕

Left and overleaf: Behind the understated decor of the living room lies a process of careful consideration and rearrangement. The dining table was made by an unnamed cabinetmaker, while the surrounding chairs are a mix of designs by Børge Mogensen and Hans J Wegner. Opposite: Originally designed for a woman, the small desk, also by Wegner, is a little too low for Christian, meaning that he rarely uses it – but he can't quite bring himself to part with it. The chair is designed by Arne Jacobsen. A range of artworks – minimalist pieces by contemporary artists and exhibition posters from Christian's favourite designers and ceramicists – decorate the walls.

Mid-Century Minimalist

There are probably not many people's first homes that look like Christian Nørgaard's apartment. Despite being only 53 square metres (570 square feet), it feels spacious – perhaps because every single item is carefully chosen with attention to design language, material and history. The interior reflects a strong sense of style and quality awareness, which isn't something you'd typically associate with a young person's apartment. 'When I visit people who've only seen photos of my home, they're often shocked that I'm not older,' says

Christian, who is 25. And visiting people is something he does quite often, as around 90 per cent of his furniture has been sourced on Facebook Marketplace, Instagram or other platforms for second-hand furniture. The main reason for this is that he prefers the original versions of old design classics, and he loves the visible signs of aging and wear and tear on the furniture – patina is a key word for Christian, who is just about to complete his education as a construction architect. 'I'm really into patina,' he says. 'The chairs we're

sitting on, for example, are a lot older than I am. It means that, occasionally, some cane needs to be replaced or a joint needs repairing. But that's possible, and it makes the chair almost indestructible. It's much more sustainable than buying new.'

Christian's interest in furniture classics began when he was just 15 years old. Back then, he often went to flea markets with his sister. As space in his bedroom grew tight with purchases, they began selling some of the things that didn't fit in or that they no longer needed. He quickly

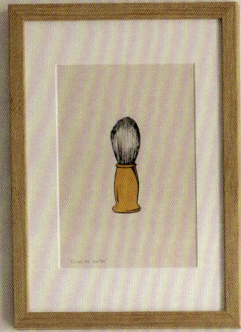

GERTRUD VASEGAARD

CLAUSENS KUNSTHANDEL

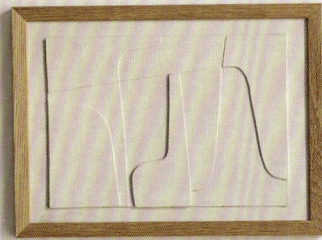

SAXBO

STENTØJ 1929–1968

2.–31. AUGUST 1975

NORDJYLLANDS KUNSTMUSEUM

realized that certain furniture from specific designers could be sold for a profit, and it all became a bit of a sport. He started buying pieces he wouldn't necessarily furnish his own home with, as long as the price was right. Around this time, he also became fascinated with Danish ceramics from the 1930s to 1960s, and he learned the names, signatures and distinctive features of some of the country's most iconic ceramic artists. Over the years, he has managed to find quite a few vases, jugs and lidded jars for significantly lower prices than their actual market value. It's the thrill of the hunt that excites him – he wouldn't dream of walking into a department store where designer furniture is lined up in rows. 'I find that a bit boring because it doesn't require much effort. It's more fun for me to have something that not just anyone can go out and buy,' he says about his collection, which has required both perseverance and luck to build. He emphasizes that the name of the designer isn't the most important thing for him – it's the superior quality and timelessness of a piece. For example, his dining table was made by an unknown cabinetmaker, but Christian fell in love with its craftmanship.

When Christian and his partner Frederik moved into their 131-year-old apartment in 2019, it wasn't exactly in poor condition, but the kitchen was worn and outdated, and its green linoleum floor had seen better days. However, renovating the space wasn't easy because of the numerous awkward angles. The existing cupboards had been custom-built to fit, and the couple ended up simply replacing the countertop and buying a new, smaller fridge to create a larger work surface in the small room. They also painted the cupboard fronts,

added new handles and put up tiles. Custom-built oak shelves, a Georg Jensen wall clock and Christian's collection of Stelton jugs in various sizes added a personal touch.

Overall, it was a challenge to furnish the apartment due to the limited square footage and the many uneven walls and angles. 'You can't just do whatever you want in such a small space. There are so many pieces of furniture I dream of getting but don't have room for, and it's been a real process to find the perfect things for the apartment – at one point, for example, we only had two chairs around the table. But I think it's important to be patient in that process. Many people think everything has to be ready at the snap of a finger. But you shouldn't surround yourself with things you don't really like just because you can't wait six months for the right item to

Above: With a few simple updates, Christian and Frederik have refreshed the old kitchen, ensuring it will last for years to come. The coffee drip kettle on the stove is from Hario Buono. Opposite: Christian has a particular appreciation of wooden and ceramic objects, and his ceramics collection has been over a decade in the making. It includes many rare pieces, especially from the Danish brand Saxbo, which was founded in 1929 and closed in 1968. Designed in 1962, the striking lamp above the dining table is Poul Henningsen's Kontrast. The sofa is by Erik Jørgensen, the CH25 chair by Hans J Wegner. The Accent side table is from the Danish brand Mater.

✕

Above and opposite: To save floor space in the narrow bedroom, the couple's wardrobe is contained within a row of IKEA wall-hung cabinets, no longer in production. With just a few well-chosen details and a focus on quality materials and a strong design language, Christian has created a sense of openness and visual calm in just 53 square metres (570 square feet). The bronzed brass candleholder with cane weaving is from Audo Copenhagen, while the coat rack and small mirror were designed by Kai Kristiansen for Aksel Kjersgaard.

come along. Instead, you could make do with some folding chairs from the basement for when guests come round,' he believes.

It doesn't take long to notice the prominent use of wood and how it defines the aesthetic of the apartment. It is Christian's favourite material, and he has a particular love of oak – not only because, in his view, it's a beautiful wood, but also because it's incredibly sturdy, making it very resilient to marks. 'It's fantastic that you can continue to work with solid wood if it shows signs of wear. You can sand it, oil it or treat it with soap. It's a very forgiving material,' says Christian. His love of oak and his knowledge of its qualities have certainly had an impact on his decision to buy used furniture rather than new. Older pieces are often made from higher-quality wood than is usually available today – trees are

typically felled much earlier now due to the increased demand for their wood. Over time, it has become more important to Christian that his furniture should be not only beautiful but also able to cope with everyday use. That's why he has replaced the dining chairs he once had with chairs made from less fragile materials. Initially, aesthetics dictated which pieces he bought but he worried that his valuable chairs would break when people sat in them. Now he's started to prioritize sturdiness. As he says, 'My home isn't a museum. Things should be able to withstand being used.'

Stories of the Past

Much more than the actual design, it is the story behind a piece of furniture that truly fascinates Niklas Søgaard. Early in his adult life, he considered studying history or art history, seeing himself working in a museum or teaching. However, when he had the opportunity to join Klassik – one of the world's leading specialist stores for vintage furniture classics – he seized it, recognizing a unique chance to work with design and heritage in a more hands-on setting. When he later met his partner Martha Menko, it turned out that they shared a deep interest in

the past, which is naturally reflected in their spacious two-room apartment.

'We surround ourselves with many things that aren't necessarily exciting in themselves, but it's the stories behind them that make them special to us,' says Niklas. One example is their sturdy sofa by Swiss manufacturer De Sede, which was in Klassik when Niklas started working there. He hated it at first. 'I didn't understand why, among the refined furniture from Finn Juhl and Hans J Wegner in the store, there was this clunky 1970s buffalo

leather thing. My boss didn't like it either. But as I learned more about the craftsmanship and history, it became increasingly alluring in my eyes,' he explains. Five or six years later, Niklas offered to buy the sofa for the couple's apartment and it came home to live with them. 'It's quite small, but you can pull the seat out, allowing both us and the dog to lie on it,' he says with a smile.

The apartment's decor has a relaxed, unpretentious style, revealing that its residents prioritize craftsmanship and personal stories over names, brands or origins

Left and far left: The tall vase was made by ceramicist Kirsten Günther at the Danish factory Knabstrup in the 1970s; the large bowl is by contemporary ceramicist Christa Julin. Opposite: Dating back to the 1970s, the large travertine dining table was bought at an antiques shop in Sweden; the surrounding chairs were designed by Danish furniture designer Poul Volther. Small, custom-made 'shoes' have been put under the chair legs to raise their height. This has been necessary because many chairs from the 1950s and '60s are quite low, as people were generally shorter then.

✕

Previous pages: Niklas and Martha's living room is defined by the large shelving system, composed of several modules, with its shelves filled with books, ceramics and collectables. Designed by Børge Mogensen and Grethe Meyer in the 1960s, the shelving unit came in multiple configurations with different features. The laminated birch lounge chair is by Alvar Aalto. This page: Throughout the interior, natural materials and warm tones take centre stage. Niklas has a particular fondness for oak, pine and Oregon pine, a wood that's not often used for contemporary furniture. The low bench is a rare model in Oregon pine by Poul Kjærholm and Jørgen Høj, designed for Bovirke in 1957. Above it, the yellow-green painting is by young Danish artist Mikkel Ørsted. The small sofa in elm and French rattan was designed by Roald Steen Hansen in 1984.

and creating a space that feels thoughtful, curated and connected to natural materials and artisanal design. Historical everyday objects like foot massagers, headrests and bowls are scattered around the floor, transformed into decorative sculptures to add an artistic dimension to the rooms and bridge the gap between functionality and aesthetics. Many were found at auction, and Niklas keeps an eye on local, national and international auction houses, where he has set up numerous search alerts for furniture designers, ceramicists and artists he's interested in. While he mainly browses online, Martha enjoys visiting flea markets and charity shops, especially in the countryside, where she has often found great bargains. 'Every time we head out of town or travel somewhere new, we do research beforehand to find out where the flea markets are,' says Martha.

For the couple, however, the experience associated with each purchase is what truly matters, which is why they appreciate their opal glass lamps – the Radiohus and China

This page: Blending in perfectly with the golden tones of the living room is the rice paper floor lamp designed by Isamu Noguchi. The small pine side table, crafted by an unknown cabinetmaker, is from the 1970s. The elm chest of drawers with recessed handles is a unique piece, designed in 1935 by Hans Christian Hansen and Viggo S Jørgensen.

pendants by Vilhelm Lauritzen and Bent Karlby respectively – hanging above the dining table and sofa. They discovered both lamps, completely covered in dust, in the bulky waste collection of their courtyard. But after a good cleaning, they looked pristine. 'We probably never would have bought either of those lamps ourselves, but they kind of found us. That's why we feel a special connection to them,' says Niklas, who, through his work, has gained extensive knowledge of how furniture was produced in the past,

and sees far greater value in things that are decades old than in their factory-new counterparts.

Niklas and Martha have similar tastes and often come across great finds, but just as often they have to persuade each other not to acquire more, especially larger pieces, as the apartment's footprint of 88 square metres (947 square feet) is limiting. This happened as recently as the day before this interview, when they fell in love with a beautiful dining table, with an oak top and steel frame, by Danish designer Piet Hein and Swedish

✕

Left: Niklas often visits ceramicists and artists in their workshops, and it was during one such visit to Hans Vangsø that he bought the yellow-green vase. Opposite: On the windowsill, the dark vase is by Jais Nielsen for Royal Copenhagen and was a gift. The woven bench was designed by Jørgen Bækmark for the furniture manufacturer FDB. An antique African headrest found at a flea market stands on the hand-woven rug from Oaxaca, Mexico. Martha is very attached to the painted dough bowls from the workshop Pottemageriet Rødeled because her grandparents owned many of its pieces.

designer Bruno Mathsson. Still, practicality doesn't always prevail. 'I sometimes get caught up in the excitement of a good buy and bid on something I don't actually need, thinking that I probably won't win the auction anyway, so no harm done, and then I end up winning it,' says Niklas. As an example, he recently bought a couple of chairs because he could not pass up the opportunity. They are now stored in the cellar because there's no room for them in the apartment. About a year ago, the couple bought a summer house in the north of Denmark. For a while, they justified new purchases by saying they could use them there, but now space is running out in the summer house, too.

While the furniture in the apartment is frequently updated, certain pieces will never be replaced. The most treasured items in Niklas's collection are his sculptures by Danish painter and ceramicist Jais Nielsen, along with a large, yellow-green vase with a rough glaze by contemporary ceramicist Hans Vangsø, prominently displayed on the bookshelf. He's so taken with the vase that he often finds himself reaching for it. As Niklas explains, 'These pieces are at the higher end of the price range, but we'd rather invest in things we can use and admire than invest in stocks – it just makes more sense to us. On the other hand, it does makes them harder to part with.'

✕TIP

People have a tendency to place all their furniture along the walls, which can create a sense of there not being enough furniture in the room. If you have a large or elongated living room, consider arranging it with several smaller seating areas within the space. If the sofa is placed against the end wall, make sure it's pulled 20–30cm (8–12in) away, to add depth, improve air circulation and make the arrangement feel more intentional. If you have the space, allow sofas, open-backed bookcases or sideboards to stand in the centre of the room, to define smaller zones.

✕

Left and opposite: The high-ceilinged rooms are tastefully furnished with classic artworks, sculptures and pieces of Danish design. Cow Horn chairs by Hans J Wegner surround the dining table by Niels Koefoed, bought at the auction house Bruun Rasmussen. Hanging over the table is the pendant lamp Septima by Poul Henningsen, now produced by Louis Poulsen. The eclectic mix of artworks are from markets and other dealers or have been painted by friends.

The Vintage Dealer's Treasury

While some play tennis and others knit, Anders and Nina Lund Forup spend most of their free time hunting for beautiful and rare furniture, lamps, art and ceramics. They are the couple behind the Danish jewellery brand HandcraftedCph and the newly opened café and vintage shop LokalCph. The couple have indulged this passion since they met 17 years ago. When they opened their first shop in 2013, their selection featured an equal mix of jewellery and vintage gems. Although having young children and work commitments have made it harder to find time to visit flea markets together, they continue to share a love for unique finds. 'Before we had kids, we went to flea markets every weekend throughout the summer, but it doesn't take long for children to start running around and pulling things off the tables. Nowadays, it's mostly Anders who goes, though I really miss it,' Nina says. Once in a while, she manages to convince their six-year-old daughter Saga to join her for a flea market trip. They wake up early, have breakfast at a nearby café, and then Saga gets

Left and opposite: In the large, oak kitchen, custom-designed shelves run along the length and around the corner of the worktop, providing space for Anders's extensive collection of teapots, coffee cups and glassware. Over the island hang pendant lamps by Poul Henningsen; the barstools are by Erik Buck. Overleaf: The living room and bookshelf displays reveal the couple's keen interest in art, particularly sculpture, which they frequently hunt for on Danish and international auction sites. Displayed side by side, the two bronze sculptures are by Knud Nellemose, who was Danish, and Taisto Martiskainen, from Finland. The green porcelain figure is by Swedish artist Arthur Percy.

a small flea market purse filled with coins to spend. 'We're trying to foster responsible consumption habits in them. After all, if there's already a well-made and solid item out there, there's no need to produce something new,' she explains.

The couple took over their 350-square-metre (3,767-square-foot) villa in 2021 and have since renovated the kitchen and bathrooms, and added elegant, built-in cupboards throughout. All the woodwork has been crafted by the carpentry firm Vermland. The style of the interior

remains entirely classic, allowing the new elements to blend seamlessly with the house's Art Nouveau-inspired architecture from 1890. The large, bright rooms are furnished with a perfectly curated mix of Nordic design classics, nameless carpentry pieces, a few modern items and a significant personal collection of handmade crafts. From basement to attic, intricately carved wooden sculptures stand side by side with bronze figures, stoneware vases and books on design and art, clearly demonstrating a deep interest in, and

a knowledge of, form, materials and history. The interior also reflects a style that is constantly evolving. A decade ago, the couple focused on renowned designers such as Hans J Wegner, Arne Jacobsen and Hvidt & Mølgaard. Today, their focus has shifted towards the era itself and they are willing to invest in lesser-known pieces from the 1930s to the 1960s, provided the craftsmanship is of high quality. 'We often buy at auction, and many auction sites start suggesting things that resemble what you've bid on before, so in that way, we often

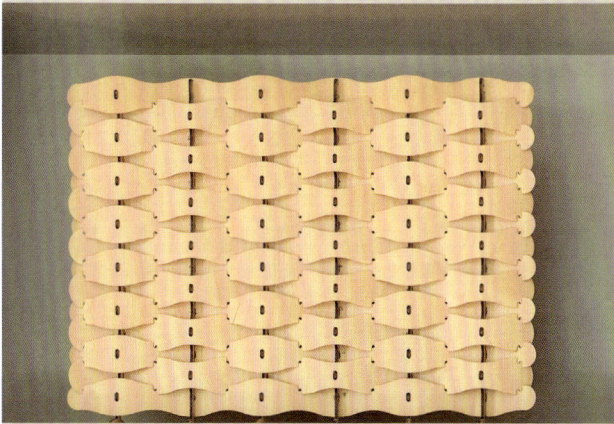

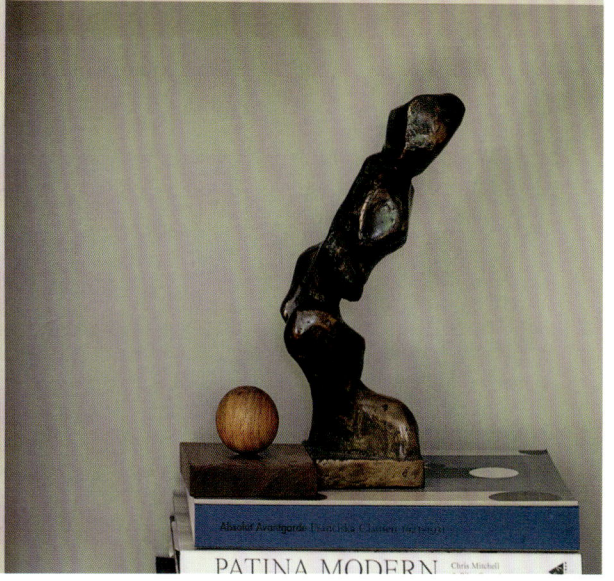

discover new names. For instance, we sometimes come across a ceramicist we didn't know before, and then we start searching more intensely for that person,' explains Nina, who primarily gets her inspiration by following furniture makers, designers, interior stylists and photographers on Instagram.

It might be hard to understand how parents dare to leave rare and valuable curiosities within arm's reach when there are two small children in the house. Yet the number of casualties in the couple's collection can be counted on one hand: when their daughter Saga was four, she decided to jump with her skipping rope indoors, which resulted in a vase hitting the floor, but otherwise, nothing has ever happened. However, they acknowledge that if you want fragile, high-end items on display, you must also be prepared for the risk of breakage. 'Of course, we keep an eye on our son Birk, but he's one and a half now and a very gentle and cautious boy, mainly interested in cars, so I think we've been lucky. Also, we don't have anything excessively pricey

Above: With a wonderful view of the garden, the living room is dedicated to relaxation and comfort. The round coffee table with club-shaped legs is quite a recent purchase. It bears no stamp or label but is attributed to furniture dealer and upholsterer Otto Færge. Designed between 1940 and 1960, the floor lamp was bought at a German auction and is likely Italian. Anders has a weakness for these cocoon lamps, whose shades showcase an innovative technique in which liquid plastic polymer was sprayed over a metal frame. The wall lamp with three shades was designed by Serge Mouille.

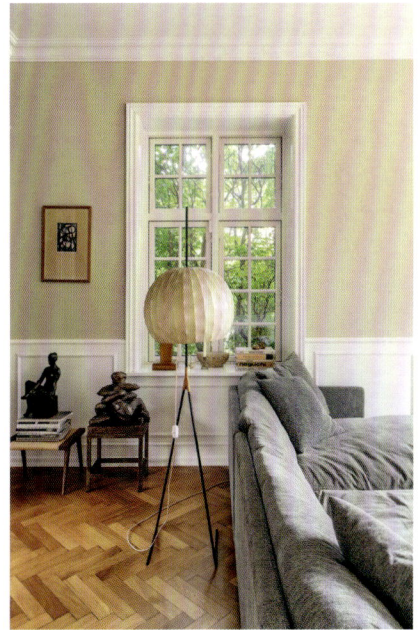

This page: Although traditional in shape, the voluminous, heavily upholstered armchairs fit seamlessly into the modern interior, thanks to their light-coloured bouclé fabric. The small lithograph alongside was bought at auction, while the wooden sculpture and Shaker boxes were discovered at various markets. In contrast to the bulky armchairs, the cotton chenille sofa from the renowned Danish brand Eilersen is sleek and low.

within their reach, as it wouldn't be fair to put our kids in a situation where they might accidentally break something,' says Nina, noting that football or similar activities indoors are obviously out of the question.

Although the interior appears both cohesive and balanced, Anders and Nina don't always agree on the direction the aesthetic should take. While Anders is a maximalist and enjoys a 'more is more' approach, Nina prefers more light and space around her, so she occasionally has to veto more knick-knacks. 'I think we've found a good balance,' she explains, 'but Anders brings something home almost every day, and every so often I have to say, "We need to talk about this corner because it's too cluttered for the vacuum to get in – is there any wiggle room here?" Then we meet in the middle,' she smiles, concluding that perhaps that's just part of living with a man who deals in vintage interiors daily and has a habit of falling in love with new pieces without necessarily having a designated spot for them. Often, furniture, lamps, art and artifacts are simply brought

home to be 'tried out' before Anders decides whether to sell them on. This can lead to seven chairs suddenly appearing around the small round table in the front hall. 'I typically look for items we actually need, like a lamp or a rug, while Anders tends to buy things first and then finds a place for them later. However, this merely reflects the inspiration he draws from surrounding himself with things he finds beautiful, which I truly value,' she explains.

With new items often brought into the house, the collection is sometimes rotated, but one piece that will always remain is the solid oak dining table by Niels Koefoed in the dining room. The couple bought it at auction, and it has moved with the family from home to home. Should the children leave a mark on it, it can be sanded down and waxed, and it's as good as new. 'We try to be very thoughtful about everything we bring into the house – and everything that leaves it as well. And that table is something neither of us has any intention of parting with – it's beautiful craftsmanship and practical, too.'

✕

Previous pages: Decorated in calming tones, the simply furnished bedroom features a large lithograph, likely by Ernst Hansen, above the rattan headboard, two vintage brass wall lamps by Vilhelm Lauritzen and a woven lounge chair by Yngve Ekström. Opposite: Like the kitchen, the oak bathroom vanity was custom-built by Vermland. Nina's great-grandmother stitched the alphabet embroidery in the children's room in 1965; the concertina coat rack was unearthed at a flea market. The table, surrounded by vintage IKEA chairs, designed by Karin Mobring, was salvaged from a bulky-waste collection and repainted.

✕ TIP

A classic oil painting can be an exciting contrast to clean lines and neutral tones. If you fall in love with a traditional painting with an imposing gold frame that doesn't quite fit with your decor, it's relatively easy to ease the canvas out of the frame. You can then either put the painting in a slimmer frame, which draws less attention, or you can use it unframed for a light, informal look.

The Language of Travel

For most people, the idea of travelling the world, experiencing different cultures and living out of a backpack, is the opposite of settling down and building a home. However, for Josias Juliussen, both lifestyles easily coexist. For as long as he can remember, he's been curious about the world, yet he's found great comfort in always being able to return to the building where he was born and has lived most of his adult life. 'Even though I enjoy travelling and living abroad, I feel a strong connection to the city I grew up in, and no matter how much fun I'm having getting lost somewhere far away, I'm always drawn back to the same place I was born,' says Josias, who has lived in three different apartments in the same building since moving away from his childhood home.

He took over the 106-square-metre (1,141-square-foot) studio on the third floor in early 2020 just before the COVID-19 lockdowns. Not being able to travel gave him the necessary peace to decorate his new home, including selecting colours – a challenging task due to the open floor plan that allows you to see all the walls in the three large rooms simultaneously. The colours had to not only complement each other but also harmonize as a whole. Some might, though, consider royal blue and egg-yolk yellow bold choices, but Josias loves the contrast between the two colours. Similarly, he loves the striking wall of weathered cast iron and glass that separates the living room and bedroom. It was installed by the apartment's previous owners, and he could never dream of removing it.

✕

Left and opposite: One end of the living room takes on a near-graphic expression due to the deep blue colour of the back wall and the green seating modules. Designed by Peter J Lassen, founder of Montana Furniture, the Gridmo modules were produced by the company in the 1990s in a range of bold colours, such as blue, yellow, green, red and black. Above: The armchair by the window is Hans J Wegner's GE290; the steel and plastic table lamp is by Verner Panton. Overleaf: Like many of the sculptures in his home, Josias bought the patterned rug while on his travels.

Josias has worked extensively in visual communication and as a photographer. His curiosity about the world has led him to deliberately pursue jobs that would take him as far away from the familiar streets of his hometown as possible. As a result, he has worked in Korea, Belgium and South Africa, and the decor of his apartment reflects his broad, international perspective.

Alongside familiar design classics like Hans J Wegner's GE290 armchair and Jean Prouvé's Standard dining chair, Josias has exciting, more artisanal finds, clearly chosen for their strong, expressive qualities, such as the round sculpture in the kitchen/dining area, which he discovered at auction. 'It's a sun mask from the Bwa tribe in Burkina Faso,' says Josias, 'and I think it blends really well with Scandinavian decor due to its bold, graphic style.' He also enjoys visiting

✕

Above and opposite above: Thanks to the cast-iron and glass partition wall, the bedroom is just as bright as the rest of the apartment. There is also room for two more Gridmo modules, while a philodendron adds a cohesive touch to the colour scheme. **Opposite below:** Throughout the space, sculptures, reliefs and small wooden figurines from distant places are used as decorative elements.

art and folk craft museums on his travels, drawing inspiration from such places as the streets of Taipei, the museums in Tokyo and the teahouses, antique stores and temples of Kyoto. 'When I travel or spend extended periods abroad, I always carry my camera. It's my way of capturing the moments and inspirations that resonate with me,' he adds.

When Josias is away for longer periods of time, he usually rents out the apartment, and when he returns and sees his home with fresh eyes, he often experiences a desire for change.

Sometimes he repaints the walls in different colours, but on one occasion, he sold most of what he owned online and bought new things that were more aligned with his ever-evolving sense of style. However, 'new' isn't exactly the right term, as almost everything is, of course, second-hand – from flea markets, auction sites and social media platforms. 'It's a fun hobby to have. I don't watch a lot of TV, but I often browse auction sites. Auctionet, Bukowskis and Pamono are some of the ones I frequent the most, and I have a lot of search agents set up

✕

Opposite: The open-plan kitchen/
dining area is a striking composition:
the streamlined Eames dining table,
paired with vintage school chairs and
Jean Prouvé's Standard chair from 1934,
contrast beautifully with the large cabinet,
small painted stool, carved shield and
drum, repurposed as a plant pedestal.
The large lithograph alongside is *Water
Drops*, a 1988 piece by South Korean artist
Kim Tschang-yeul. Verner Panton's Moon
pendant hangs over the table. Above: The
kitchen area in the apartment had already
been renovated when Josias moved in.
To add warmth to the simple, modern
elements, he uses Spanish terracotta tapas
bowls for storing fruit and vegetables.
A classic Danish rye bread slicer from
Raadvad stands alongside. Produced in
large numbers from 1905 to 1980, the
slicer is still widely available in Danish
charity shops today.

there,' says Josias. One of his best tips
for scoring great deals at auctions is
to expand the search criteria a little.
For example, instead of searching for
the well-known Togo sofa from Ligne
Roset, try the furniture company that
produces the items you are after.
'That way, you will come across other
great designs by amazing designers
that you perhaps didn't know about,'
he explains.

Josias's most valued vintage find
is the wooden cabinet in the kitchen/
dining area, which he bought from an
antique dealer on Instagram. It was
built by Swedish artist and furniture
maker Eugen Höglund in the 1950s.
What catches the eye are the doors,
which are adorned with panels
depicting the world's continents,
bar Antarctica, which, likely due to
symmetry or lack of space, didn't
make the cut. Josias adores bold,
voluminous expression, which he

thinks fits nicely into a modern decor
when used in controlled doses. Paired
with sleek designs like the Segmented
dining table by Eames, and Pierre
Chapo's S31 stool, the curves and
cutouts of the cabinet bring warmth
and softness to the large, open space.
Here and there, curious finds from
Josias's many travels ensure that
the atmosphere doesn't become
too trend oriented, and at the same
time, they remind him of all the great
experiences that have shaped him as
a person. As he puts it: 'My apartment
has quietly become a reflection of the
things I've experienced. I've tried to
bring a bit of the world home with me.'

Countryside Romance

When Anne Thorlund and her husband Michael were house-hunting three years ago, it was important to them that the property retained some original features, reflecting its history. Not wanting to take on a full renovation, they focused on finding homes that had been well maintained by their owners. And that's exactly what they found in the charming residence from 1904 that was once a stable and gatekeeper's lodge for the main house in the grounds opposite. The property had been renovated carefully and respectfully, using solid,

long-lasting materials, which meant not much work was needed when the couple moved in. All they did was extend the kitchen, which they then painted, and replace the cold, tiled kitchen floor with solid pine boards.

Anne is the one who wields the paintbrush, and besides painting the kitchen and the walls, she has transformed countless pieces of furniture found at flea markets, charity shops, resale platforms and during her travels. She is a trained art and crafts teacher and has always enjoyed working on creative projects.

This page: Anne loves upcycling and mixing materials. The glass lamp has been revived with a new fabric shade, and some of the small framed pictures are made from leftover fabric or wallpaper. The stool was painted and upholstered with fabric to match that of the Carimate armchair by Vico Magistretti. Although a lot of Anne's furniture comes from different eras, the pieces blend harmoniously thanks to a subdued colour palette. Opposite: New linen covers from Bemz refresh the old IKEA sofa and chaise longue. The coffee table came from a local antiques shop, the rug from Morocco.

✕

Previous pages and opposite: Surrounding the IKEA dining table, which has been given a coat of white paint, are Hans J Wegner's Wishbone Chairs, Børge Mogensen's Folkestolen and vintage children's chairs from Trip Trap (now Skagerak). The pendant lamps, bought online from TinyTiny, are made of cotton voile. This page: When Anne and her husband bought the house, the beautifully crafted kitchen was already there but they have since added an extension, which they painted to continue the colour scheme. Many of the platters as well as the chopping boards were found in antique shops in Spain and Italy, while others were bought second-hand in Denmark. The white oyster plates on the wall were discovered at flea markets.

During her maternity leave, Anne started making lamps and fabric pinboards, eventually selling her creations to private clients. 'I've always been very creative. I'm not afraid to blend styles, and I don't really mind that my belongings are from different periods,' Anne says. For instance, the family's dining table is a second-hand IKEA model that she painted a light grey. With young children in the house, the couple preferred not to invest in anything overly expensive, and they saw no reason to buy a brand-new table when they could find a preowned one. Anne's only rule of thumb is that textiles, such as napkins and towels, should be new. However, that rule can be broken, as shown by the striped curtains in the kitchen, created by textile designer Helene Blanche. They were acquired from a lady who needed to part with them because she was moving home; when new, they would have been beyond their budget.

It's not just the financial benefits that drive the couple's preference for buying second-hand. Anne also loves the fact that these belongings come with a story. 'Things hold more value for me when they have a story. But it requires the ability to see their potential, even if they may appear unattractive at first,' she explains, recalling how she once returned to a local charity shop six times before deciding whether to buy an old stool that had caught her eye. Made of dark wood with a crocheted seat marred by stains, it wasn't exactly a bargain at the price. Nevertheless, she ultimately took it home, sanded it down, painted it light grey and re-covered it with a beautiful piece of fabric she already

This page: On the upper floor, the slanted walls and white-painted beams create a cosy and intimate feel in the bedroom. The lovely pleated lampshade made by Anne has given the bedside lamp a new lease of life. Opposite: Bunting, artwork and a mobile decorate the children's room, inviting play. The small table on the rug from Roomers & Woodbox was made by a local carpenter. The child's Hukit chair is from the 1970s; the J81 woven chair is by Jørgen Bækmark for FDB. Next up for renovation is the bathroom. Over the mirror is a Jieldé wall lamp; the woven stool is from Culture Living.

had. Today, it is unrecognizable. 'For me, the decision-making process takes time, and that can be risky when it comes to a vintage item that is one of a kind. It's a balance I'm learning to navigate. If the item I've fallen in love with is in a shop, I try to leave it for a week before deciding. If it's at a flea market, I might only give it an hour,' she says with a smile.

The calm, coordinated and harmonious home reflects the presence of someone with a keen eye for aesthetics – but it is particularly thanks to Michael that surfaces aren't cluttered with items. 'We're both collectors, but he's definitely more organized about it. If it weren't for him, I would have gone mad – I often have four different projects on the go at the same time. However, I've become better at assessing what I can make myself and what fits my style,' says Anne. While Michael is a craftsman with a fondness for high-quality windows, doors and other building materials that others have discarded, she has a similar soft spot for plates, woven baskets and picture frames. The craftsmanship of the old frames appeals to her, resulting in her entire wardrobe being filled with frames tucked behind clothes. They don't just gather dust, however; they are transformed into decorative bulletin boards whenever she has time to work on her crafts.

Side by side with local vintage finds are souvenirs from the family's travels, including trips to France and Italy. The decor has a charmingly relaxed and effortless quality, but the truth is that achieving this style has taken years of practice. 'I've previously brought home some

Left and opposite: In the hallway, a space difficult to furnish because of its function, Anne has made good use of the long wall to create a working area. She designed and covered the pinboard herself with fabric. All the bowls and cups were found at various flea markets across Denmark and southern Europe.

peculiar items from our travels. For instance, we've been to Japan a few times because Michael has family there, and you really need to be careful; the atmosphere can easily sweep you away. Now I know from bitter experience that, regardless of how cool Koinobori streamers and Kokeshi dolls look in other people's homes, they just don't work for me,' Anne says with a laugh. Today, she researches in advance what the locals in the country she visits are especially good at making, and then she might make some purchases. These could be pots or jugs made from a very specific type of clay found only in that particular region. She has discovered that it helps to have pictures of her home on her phone, which she holds up alongside the item she has fallen in love with. This way, she can quickly see if it will fit in. 'We've just been to Mallorca, where I bought some copper prints from an artist, and it was actually quite difficult to make a decision while not at home, but I think it turned out well.'

✕ TIP

Seventy years ago, modular sofas with lounging sections and chaises longues didn't exist – sofas were designed for sitting up straight – so having an older sofa today may mean compromising on comfort. Additionally, many vintage seating pieces are now worn from years of use and may require (costly) reupholstering. Fortunately, it's quite possible to find new sofas with a similar look, and several furniture companies offer options like tapered legs in various wood types to suit a mid-century modern style. Choose a subdued colour for the upholstery, such as grey or beige, and add cushions made from vintage fabric to tie the style together.

The Potter's Penthouse

If you say the word 'rectory', most people probably wouldn't picture Katrine Blinkenberg and Morten Sternberg's airy Copenhagen apartment in the futuristic Metropolis building, with sea surrounding on all sides. However, the couple are both trained theologians – though only Morten continues to work as a parish priest. Katrine left the ministry three years ago to become a self-taught artist, and since then, she has not only created her own sculptures but taught others how to work artistically with clay and plaster. 'I had never created anything with my hands before, but the only thing I wanted to do was make a sculpture. I didn't have a ceramic kiln, so I used plaster, as it doesn't need to be fired. After many attempts, I succeeded. Right away, although I was really nervous, I began teaching it, and three months later, I had my first exhibition,' Katrine says. Much of her teaching takes place in the couple's apartment, which is furnished with sturdy furniture and minimal knick-knacks. This way, there's less to clean – both after Katrine's students and the couple's two boys. 'We use our home a lot, and it is also my workplace. Therefore, there shouldn't be too much that distracts the eye or too much to keep tidy. My belongings already take up plenty of space in the landscape. I actually prefer my home to feel a bit more like a monastery cell,' says Katrine with a laugh.

Despite its modernity, the apartment's design lacked warmth and tactility, prompting the couple to be mindful of their interior choices. As a result, most of their furniture, lamps, art and tableware have

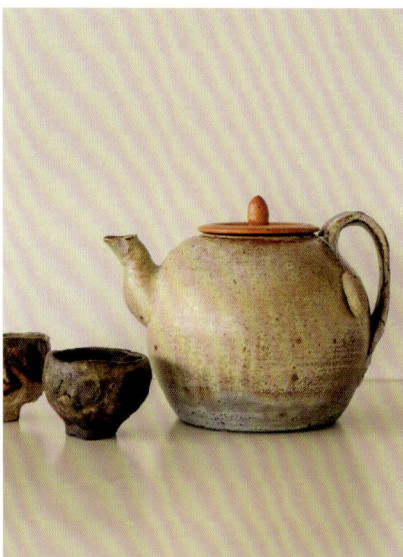

✕

Opposite and overleaf: Around the large pine table stand vintage examples of Børge Mogensen's Folkestol and Peter Ole Schiønning's Safari chair. Isamu Noguchi's Akari paper lanterns hang over the table; the vase is one of Katrine's own creations. Left: The canvas of the Safari chairs was originally stretched tightly between the two side rails, but after years of supporting many backs, it has started to sag slightly, which is fine with Katrine – she likes to see that her things have been put to good use. Far left: Katrine also made the cups on the countertop.

been sourced second-hand, with a purposeful selection of natural materials like wood, leather, canvas and stoneware. They rarely buy anything new – primarily because they prefer not to fill the very sparse, minimalist space with new things, but also because they've been fortunate enough to save a lot of money by hunting down preowned design classics. For instance, they acquired the two Akari paper lamps by Isamu Noguchi for the dining table from a 'Trusted Seller' on eBay at a fraction of the recommended retail price. Although it can be challenging to find good furniture deals online due to high shipping costs, the fact that the lamps could be packed flat eliminated that concern. However, Katrine still prefers sourcing her pieces at actual markets, where she can touch everything that catches her eye. As a ceramicist, her hands are her most

reliable tool, making it essential for her to feel each item before deciding if it's something she should bring home. 'We've found that the atmosphere in here would become far too cold and hostile if we just filled the rooms with new things – there's a need to soften the hard lines,' Katrine explains, noting that she has also added several natural fibre rugs to enhance the acoustics. It does, though, still echo in the large living room, and Katrine plans to create a wall hanging for the long hallway to help absorb some sound. Over the years, she has collected various fabrics that she intends to sew together into a single large piece.

Her interest in hunting for vintage pieces began when she was motivated by limited resources during her studies. She was inspired by a classmate who had a knack for discovering treasures at flea

✕

Above left: The apartment's furniture has been sourced from all over – from bulky waste collections, flea markets and second-hand shops to auction sites, Instagram profiles and eBay listings. Some pieces have also been gifts or purchases from friends in the art and design trade. Katrine found the almost brutalist chair on Facebook Marketplace, buying it from the maker's daughter. Above right: Her ceramic tools are scattered around as decorative elements. Opposite: Katrine made the ceramic sculptures, glazed with crushed stones from Ukraine. The table lamp in the corner was found on a Swedish auction site and is likely a Stilnovo model from the 1940s. Overleaf: Curvaceous and compact, the sofa from Sofacompany is one of the few pieces in the apartment bought new. The two folding lounge chairs in full-grain leather are a J Hardy design; the coffee table is by Andreas Hansen.

markets and had created a beautifully decorated home for herself. When Katrine moved out of the city and into her first rectory, she suddenly found herself in need of far more furniture than she had assembled in her small student accommodation. The first thing she did was visit the local charity shops. 'It started out of necessity, but it quickly turned into a passion,' she says. Now, in her role as a creator, and as someone who helps others in their creative endeavours, she can't help but appreciate the appearance and sensation an item takes on after being in someone else's hands. For this reason, she has no desire to surround herself with items that come directly from a factory, as they seem devoid of history in her eyes. In contrast, a preloved piece of furniture always carries a story with it, even if she doesn't know what it is. 'To me, an object becomes much more beautiful when it has been touched by a human being, because I believe that humans are one of the most wonderful things in existence,' says Katrine, adding that you can learn a great deal from observing how people work with their hands. She can tell, for example, when someone is stressed; it manifests in

their inability to control their hands, which causes their creations to fall apart. 'Sometimes people come to my home thinking they are going to relax, but then they have to sit still for two or three hours, which they simply can't do. It often happens that my guests end up crying because it opens up different conversations when you're not just staring at each other but are instead focused on what you're creating. In reality, I'm still doing emotional support work. That's why it's important for me to have my own practice, where it's calm and pleasant to be,' she says.

Now having everything they need for the 128-square-metre (1,378-square-foot) apartment, the couple don't replace anything until it eventually falls apart. As a result, interior design is more or less a completed chapter for Katrine, and although she enjoys being surrounded by things she finds beautiful, she has no emotional attachment to any of her belongings. 'Occasionally, the children break some of my sculptures by accident, which is unfortunate if it's a piece created by one of my clients; otherwise, I don't mind. It's only people that I care about in that way.'

Opposite above right and below left: In the bedroom and children's rooms, Katrine and Morten have had elevated beds built, to create more storage space as well as making the most of the spectacular view, especially when falling asleep and waking up. Opposite above left: In a corner of the kitchen stands another Safari chair, alongside a large lithograph by the Danish artist Mogens Andersen. Opposite below right: As in many modern apartments, the bathroom is fairly anonymous, but a vase and a small artwork add a personal touch to the space.

✕ TIP

Mixing furniture of different shapes can be a good idea, especially if the architecture of your home is very linear. If all the furniture in a square room is also square, the space can feel less lively. So, for example, if your dining table is rectangular, opt for a round coffee table and perhaps a sofa with soft, rounded edges.

Wood, Wicker and Velvet

Sharp lines, warm tones and an abundance of oak define the style of Jesper Finderup and Stine Gosvig's 1967 home. Three years ago, when they bought the house – originally a functionalist villa with a flat roof – they had the clear goal of preserving as much of the original character as possible. However, shortly after moving in, extensive water damage forced them to replace the original parquet flooring and all the plumbing, which led to the removal of the two 1980s bathrooms. Despite this comprehensive renovation, they managed to retain several original details. The new elements were carefully chosen from classic materials that blend beautifully with the house's architectural style, ensuring durability for generations. 'We wanted to stay true to the period, so we opted for classic 15 x 15-cm [6 x 6-in] tiles in the bathrooms, but added

a twist by combining three colours. To create cohesion between the different rooms, we chose oak, brass and natural stone as the consistent materials,' says Jesper. He is the co-founder and creative director of the slow fashion brand Forét, while Stine works in marketing, communications and styling at the furniture design company NORR11, which is known particularly for its minimalist bouclé sofas and lounge chairs.

The villa's 149 square metres (1,604 square feet) clearly reflect a couple with a refined sense of aesthetics, design and colour combinations. The soft hues on the walls, combined with the many wooden pieces of furniture, create a warm and inviting atmosphere. Yet there are a few bolder elements that break the serene expression, such as the coral-coloured doors, contemporary artworks and dark,

Opposite: In Jesper and Stine's charming brick house, it is all the small elements in natural materials, like stoneware, woven fibres and warm wood, that create the atmosphere. Designed by Paolo Rizzatto in 1973, the 265 model wall lamp from Flos has its shade directed over the Hans J Wegner coffee table. Above left: The stool with club-shaped legs was designed by Swedish maker Ingvar Hildingsson in the 1970s. Above right: In front of the beautiful and original stained glass window stands a small collection of Dalahästar. These traditional carved and painted statues of horses have been produced in Sweden since the 18th century and are still made today. Overleaf: The velvet sofa is from Eilersen, with scatter cushions by Danish brand Studio Feder. The leather lounge chair is Børge Mogensen's Spanish chair.

patinated oak panels. These were revealed when they removed the wallpaper in the dining room. Like the stained-glass windows, they are a charming relic from the 1960s, which they couldn't bear to discard. 'When the light filters through the coloured glass, it creates an almost rainbow-like play on the ceiling, which only recently caught our daughter Olga's attention,' Stine explains.

Neither she nor Jesper grew up in design-conscious homes. For Jesper, the fascination with vintage began with mopeds, which he started buying and selling while still living at home with his parents. When he moved out, his interest shifted to tables. 'While my friends spent their time watching football, I was searching for furniture,' Jesper says. For Stine, it was a matter of not being able to afford expensive designer furniture while she was studying. Before they

Above: Everyone in Jesper and Stine's circle thinks they should tear down the conservatory because it blocks light into the living room, but they love the space, as it extends the summer season at both ends. The couple were told that the stackable woven chairs by Hans J Wegner originally stood in the B&W Halls, a former industrial complex on the outskirts of Copenhagen. Opposite above: Muller Van Severen designed the distinctive green wall lamp, while the children's bench is by Kaare Klint. The rug is from Nordic Knots. Opposite below: In a corner, a rice paper lamp by Isamu Noguchi is paired with a narrow bookcase by an unknown cabinetmaker. Propped up against the wall is a lithograph by the Danish artist Frederik Næblerød.

became parents, finding vintage gems online and at flea markets to resell for a profit became almost a hobby, and for a few years, they even ran a sales profile on Instagram. But since Olga's arrival, time has been limited, so now they primarily use their treasure-hunting skills to find furniture, lamps and ceramics for their home.

And they're in no rush. Both are patient by nature and enjoy the thrill of the hunt for the perfect piece of furniture at the right price. For example, the shelving system at the end of the dining table, like the table itself, was designed by Danish furniture designer Børge Mogensen. It comprises several shelves, sideboards and drawers, all acquired for next to nothing at auctions over the years. 'Sometimes you get lucky and find something really cheap at auction because there aren't other eager buyers when the hammer falls.

In that way, you can secure a better deal than when buying from private sellers, who may have googled the item beforehand and set the price based on the highest figure they could find,' Jesper explains. He has numerous alert agents on auction sites as well as resale platforms for private sellers, mainly to monitor price trends on items of interest. This way, when something exciting comes up, he knows straightaway whether the price is fair. For instance, he had kept an eye on sofas from the highly sought-after Danish furniture producer Eilersen. When a reasonably priced one finally appeared, he knew he had to act quickly, and he arranged with the seller to collect the sofa the same day. Upon his arrival, the seller informed him that four other people had offered higher prices. 'At that time, we were students with very

limited funds. However, we felt we couldn't turn it down, as we had wanted it for so long,' Jesper recalls.

The couple particularly enjoy buying vintage furniture that's made of wood and wicker because they are materials that develop a special glow over years of use. Jesper even regrets having bought the Børge Mogensen and Hans J Wegner lounge chairs new instead of waiting for them to turn up on the second-hand market. 'It takes a surprisingly long time for the furniture to acquire that golden patina. We've had the Spanish chair for five years now, and the wood and leather still look new. I've even thought of swapping them for older, patinated versions, but that seems a bit silly,' he admits.

As Stine and Jesper's understanding of design and design history has deepened, they have developed a greater interest in exploring diverse styles and expressions. For many years, they have primarily surrounded themselves with design from the Danish masters of the 1960s. However, as these pieces have become more prevalent in many homes, they are now looking to discover unique items that bring

Opposite and above right: The couple's love of oak and Danish design is especially evident in the dining room. Surrounding the Shaker table by Børge Mogensen are well-worn versions of the J81 chair, designed by Jørgen Bækmark for FDB Møbler in the 1950s. On the table stands a vase by floral artist Tage Andersen. The shelving system by Børge Mogensen and Grethe Meyer was bought inexpensively at auction and gradually assembled piece by piece. Above left: The kitchen by Stillark features open shelves facing the living area, ideal for displaying cups, bowls and other fine ceramics.

Below: Alvar Aalto's classic stool brings warmth and personality to the newly renovated bathroom. Opposite: The bedrooms also feature second-hand finds, including a small teak writing module from the 1950s, Hans J Wegner's three-legged Heart chair and a large Kai Kristiansen mirror. On the dining room windowsill, a candlestick and a paper-and-oak table lamp, by Alexander Kirkeby and Atelier Axo respectively, add character. The couple's fondness for Japan is evident in their pairing of Danish design with Japanese ceramics and wooden Kokeshi dolls, which appear throughout their home. Originating in northern Japan in the Edo period (1603–1868), Kokeshi dolls were first made as children's toys but have since become collectable folk art.

a distinct character not commonly found among their social circle. They recently returned from Italy, where they were really inspired and are now in search of Italian design they can adapt for their home. 'Italian design is bolder, there's more volume, which might suit our house well, since it is very boxy, much like a lot of Danish design,' Stine explains. She adds that they're also inspired by how southern European interior designers are less afraid to mix different types of wood, including darker and heavier varieties. 'Over the years, we've turned down many heirlooms because they didn't align with our style. However, we now have a different perspective and believe they could fit in nicely. This reflects how our home is constantly evolving; it's never a snapshot of our taste and style, as we've already moved on in our minds.'

⚹TIP

A great way to create balance in a home filled with vintage furniture is with contemporary art – bold colours and abstract forms will introduce life and energy. Ensure there is plenty of space around the artworks so they don't feel overwhelming, and let the furniture serve as a subtle backdrop that enhances the art.

Vintage with a View

The interior of Inger Grubbe's spacious two-storey apartment is defined by an almost ascetic simplicity. The walls are white, the furniture is wooden and mainly in natural tones, and nothing competes with the view for attention. This, together with the impressive ceiling height, enormous windows and abundant natural light, creates a near cathedral-like atmosphere. It suits Inger well; working in a creative field, she doesn't need to be visually overstimulated in her free time. 'We don't have much on the walls because the architecture itself is so striking that it feels important to have calm spaces with large, bare surfaces where thoughts can flow freely.'

The apartment is situated in one of Copenhagen's most remarkable buildings, popularly referred to as 'The Snake' due to its organically curved facades and copper-clad roof that wind through the landscape like a serpent. Designed by the Danish artist, sculptor and performance artist Bjørn Nørgaard and built between 2004 and 2006, it's challenging to link the structure to any specific architectural period because of its distinctive character. Inger moved in with her husband Patrick and their two boys just over three years ago, but she fell in love with the building many years before while training to become a goldsmith – she used to cycle past it every day on her way to college. 'When the COVID-19 pandemic closed our children's schools, we cycled around the city, and one day we ended up here. The weather was beautiful, so we went for a walk, and I just felt that this was where I wanted to live,' she recalls.

Left: Second-hand candlesticks sit alongside the Alvar Aalto glass vase. Far left: Treasures, including ceramics, stones, a glass paperweight and a candleholder, which Inger made herself, are displayed in a typesetter's tray. Opposite: Her favourite corner is furnished with a classic lounge chair by an unknown Danish cabinetmaker. Overleaf: Inger enjoys playing with contrasts, as with light wooden furniture against dark artworks. Difficult to pair with other pieces, the large oil painting needs plenty of space around it and has an entire wall to itself. The tall woven chair is by Yngve Ekström.

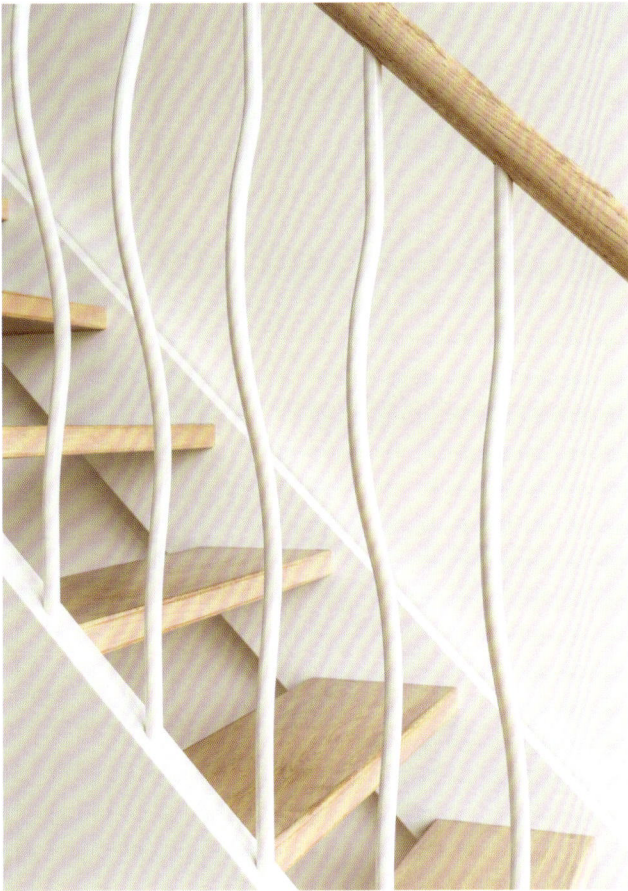

✕

Opposite: The laminate surfaces of the Alvar Aalto dining table and chairs make them especially practical for a household with young children. For the same reason, these pieces are excellent to buy second-hand – both the surfaces and the moulded birch construction are highly resistant to wear. Above left and right: Even the staircase spindles reflect the fact that the building was designed by an artist. Their flowing lines are echoed in the two-seater sofa by Rud Thygesen and Johnny Sørensen.

Inger holds a bachelor's degree in art history, which might explain why she feels so at home in a building shaped by an artist, but she didn't thrive at university. After having her first child, she chose a completely different and more practical path. It was somewhat by chance that she pursued goldsmithing but quickly realized it suited her well not to be in her head all the time and that her intelligence was really in her hands. At long last, she felt that she had found her true calling, and after being on maternity leave with her second child, she decided to start her own business as a self-employed goldsmith. 'It was only possible because my husband had finished his degree and secured his first proper job, and even today, it's far from a case of us being flush with cash,' she explains. Finances were also a major reason why she began buying second-hand, and it remains a motivation for the couple today, although it's also important to them that their belongings have a story. 'It's never been an option to walk into an interiors shop and buy a new piece of furniture, so that door has never been opened. It is also incredibly important to me that my furniture, my art and my clothes carry the stories and soul of their previous owners and the hands they have touched. The soulful aspect is quite meaningful to me, and I almost always develop a relationship with my belongings because, for me, they are animated – especially the handmade items. Therefore, not much changes in our home from year to year,' she says.

The interior is characterized by a profound appreciation for Nordic minimalism and functionality, and features iconic classics from Alvar Aalto, Arne Jacobsen, Hans J Wegner, Rud Thygesen and Swedese.

Left: The modern and rather impersonal kitchen is given character by Arne Jacobsen's iconic Ant chair – Inger's parents gave her a pair of them when she left home – and an exhibition poster that picks up on the red and blue tones of the artwork in the living room. Opposite: In the bedroom, Inger has created a workspace where collectables are displayed like a small, curated altar. The blue and white vase on top of the cabinet, from an antique shop, was a farewell gift from Inger's father before he passed away from cancer last year. The teapot is from her childhood home, which she was allowed to take with her when she moved out. Danish ceramicist Inge Marie Fruelund made the blue cup alongside. As well as holding books and records, the shelving in the living room is home to Inger's loom and sewing supplies, pieces of art and small decorative objects. It is one of the few pieces in the home that was bought new, and Inger still recalls the strange feeling of unwrapping the shelves from their bubble wrap.

The light wood contrasts beautifully with the black surfaces, while the architectural foliage plants introduce visual variation. The furniture has been carefully curated over time, creating a personal and timeless style that mirrors the couple's evolution and taste. Although their furniture carries prominent names, they are less concerned with designers and brands and more focused on avoiding excessive matching. 'If everything you furnish with is, for example, from the '70s, it looks as if you've bought it all at once over a summer. Things should ideally be added gradually, otherwise it feels too coordinated,' Inger explains. She is, in fact, a collector who finds great joy in beautiful objects, though this is only subtly reflected in the apartment's sparsely furnished rooms. One such detail is a typesetter's tray of curiosities in Inger's favourite spot – the window corner of the living room – where she sits, gazing out at the trees and watching the trains pass by. From this vantage point, she can see the sunrise, feel the weather and observe the changing seasons and colours.

When artist Bjørn Nørgaard modelled the first version of the building in clay, he drew inspiration from music, with the wavy roof representing rhythm, the brickwork the bass, the variety of windows the treble, and the doorways the pauses. This is a sensation that can be truly experienced while residing in the building. 'There really is a melody to this structure, as if everything vibrates together in some strange way,' Inger confides.

✕

Left: Trine often spends her summers within Denmark, and wherever she goes, she makes sure to visit at least a couple of flea markets – she's always on the lookout for vintage plaster figurines. Alongside her collection of hagstones (stones with naturally occurring holes) from the beach on Fanø, her figurines decorate the shelves of the display cabinet, which she painted herself. Opposite: Almost everything in the living room was bought second-hand. The rocking chair is by Illum Wikkelsø, the coffee table by Nissen & Gehl for Aksel Kjersgaard. Overleaf: One of the latest additions to the living room is the brass lamp by Egon Hillebrand, designed in the 1940s. Trine found it in her favourite second-hand shop on the mainland. She has become good friends with the shop's owners, who often tip her off when they get particularly special items in stock.

On Island Time

Although the distance between the Danish mainland and the small island of Fanø takes only 12 minutes to travel, it feels like you're entering a quieter, calmer world. The smell of the salty air, the sound of seagulls and the sight of the vast, immense sea help ease the mind and slow the heartbeat. As you step off the ferry and wander through the charming streets, you soon come across Trine Frausing's beautiful house, constructed in 1892 and comfortably perched on a small elevation. Originally built as a captain's villa,

over the last century it has been used for various businesses, including a vacuum cleaner shop, and at one point it was divided into two separate rental units. Since Trine and her husband Peter acquired the property three years ago, they have been working to restore it to its former glory, taking it room by room, with only the sitting room and the exterior left to complete.

The house holds a special place in Trine's heart because she often visited it as a young girl – she went to school on the mainland with one

of the children from the family that used to live there. Trine grew up on the mainland but moved to the island 22 years ago when she and Peter bought a house just across the road. It was a more typical Fanø house, characterized by small rooms and low ceilings, but the couple, who enjoy hosting friends and family, began longing for a home with more space and light. When they spotted a 'For Sale' sign in the window while on one of their walks, they quickly arranged a viewing. 'The basics were in place, but the house needed a major overhaul.

Opposite: Walls in white and neutral shades, together with natural materials such as oak, pine and stone, create a calm, serene atmosphere. Trine made the tall ceramic vase on the dining table; the low brass candlestick is by Robynn Storgaard. The two metal boxes alongside were found in second-hand shops. Trine has a particular fondness for plaster and stoneware heads, and her eye is always drawn to them when browsing flea markets. The tall brass candlestick was made by Torben Ørskov in the early 1960s; the vase is by an unknown ceramicist. Right and overleaf: Hans J Wegner's Wishbone chairs and two old safari chairs, inherited from Trine's mother-in-law, surround the modern dining table – a timeless mix of vintage and modern.

'We gave ourselves two years for the renovation. Three have now passed, and we're still not finished. But we wanted to take it slow, avoid rushing and renovate as sustainably as possible,' says Trine, who's a trained decorator and has worked creatively all her life, now as a self-employed visual storyteller through her company, Trine Frausing Studio.

The couple's unhurried approach is especially evident in the kitchen, a solid pine design dating back to the 1970s, which they decided to restore rather than replace. Doing the work, though, wasn't straightforward; all the doors needed to be re-veneered, and a new cabinet and plinth had to be built to accommodate a modern fridge and dishwasher. Fortunately, the manufacturer, Uno Form, still had all the original handles in stock, allowing the couple to blend modern conveniences with respect for traditional craftsmanship and aesthetics. Not everything has been preserved, but nothing has gone to waste. When they moved in, the kitchen walls were decorated with distinctive old Fanø tiles, but Trine knew they weren't an original feature of the house, which felt odd to her, so she put them up for sale. Two buyers expressed interest – one whom she knew made a living from buying and reselling, and another who owned a small, traditional house on the island's southern tip, where she planned to install them. Choosing to sell these rare and unique tiles to the latter buyer was an easy decision.

At first glance, it may not be apparent that many of the furnishings and accessories in the 209-square-metre (2,250-square-foot) home were acquired second-hand, as Trine has a knack for mixing vintage finds and heirlooms with modern pieces in a simple, timeless manner. The dining table, for example, consists of a birch plywood top with a linoleum surface and a pair of white-lacquered metal trestles from HAY.

Growing up with parents who saved for years to afford quality furniture, she developed a keen eye

✕

Left: Trine masters the art of understated, tactile contrasts. Opposite: When the couple's teenage boys asked for a fitness room, Trine began searching for vintage gym equipment that she could bear to have in her home. The luggage rack and bin had been salvaged from a train carriage. The cabinet with glass shelves was the first piece the couple bought for the house. Even though the old school lockers have been built into the wall, Trine would take them with her if they were to move home again. The cosy, pale pink bathroom is designed in a light and simple style with an oak vanity unit and brass fittings.

for craftsmanship. As a young girl, she started going to flea markets with her classmates, and occasionally she had her own stall, an activity she still enjoys. 'On the island, we have many roadside stalls, which we somewhat macabrely call "dead flea markets" because they're unmanned. There's no need to worry about theft here; no one even locks their doors or bikes,' Trine explains.

She has a keen eye for great deals and keeps a mental list of sought-after pieces – like a wooden hand mirror from the 1960s by Swedish designer Hans-Agne Jakobsson – but she also values the sense of history that comes with preowned items. 'When I buy something, I always ask about their origin, and when I sell something I've treasured, I like to pass on its story. It makes letting go a little easier.'

Both Trine and Peter are selective when it comes to buying new, and only do so after careful consideration and research. Currently, they're debating whether to replace the living room sofa, which they bought years ago from a fellow islander for about £30 ($37). Trine vividly recalls when she was furnishing her first apartment and went with her mother and Peter – who was her boyfriend at the time – to one of the many chain stores selling anonymous, trend-based furniture and accessories. 'I ended up feeling so physically unwell that I had to sit outside. It felt completely wrong to go into a furniture store and spend a small fortune there,' she remembers. 'It felt like such overconsumption, and I couldn't connect with it at all.'

✕TIP

When incorporating vintage items into your home, it often helps to disregard what they were originally intended for. A beautiful chair that's too unsteady or soft-backed to use at the dining table can instead serve as a side chair by your wardrobe, as a bedside table or as a plant stand. In the same way, vintage chocolate moulds, salt bowls and ashtrays can make lovely jewellery dishes, just as old wooden reels or glass paperweights can create an inspiring still life on a desk.

✕

Left and opposite: In the lounge, the raw architecture complements the furniture made of powder-coated steel, marble and patinated oak. The wall lamp and slatted chair are prototypes designed by Laura, while the daybed is a family heirloom. Overleaf: Also designed as bookshelves, the original windowsills in the seating area set off Laura's prototype coffee table beautifully. The bamboo chair and children's bench were bought second-hand, while the large candlestick and glass vase on the dining table are from the Forma series by Holmegaard.

Yellow Brick House

'An uncut diamond' is how designer Laura Lange describes the small yellow-brick house she and her husband Mark discovered three and a half years ago after an exhausting search for a home in the area. They were immediately captivated by the expansive window facing the garden and the abundance of original 1960s details. On a whim, they decided to arrange a viewing, even though the asking price was far beyond their budget. After wandering through the garden and peeking inside the windows, they called the estate agent.

Both felt a strong connection to the house, even without knowing how they could make it work. 'We couldn't afford it at all,' Laura recalls, 'but then the war in Ukraine broke out, the housing market stagnated and prices dropped.' The couple made several offers and, despite competition from other buyers, eventually managed to secure it at a price within their reach. The house had only had one previous owner. After the sale was finalized, the son of the elderly man who had lived there visited them, bringing along folders of old drawings and

sharing childhood memories. 'You could say we received the house's full manual – along with all its stories,' Laura says.

While some might have decided to embark on a full-scale renovation of the 60-year-old villa, Laura and Mark opted for a more considered approach. They sanded the floors, added plasterboard to stabilize a slightly loose ceiling, replaced the open fireplace with an inset one, to eliminate draughts, and removed the wallpaper, filling cracks and painting. The end result: a bright and inviting

✕

This page: For Laura, the design of their vintage dining table is so universal that it almost disappears – but in a good way. The Torno aluminium chairs are by +Halle; the woollen rug is from Kusiner Carpets. Laura doesn't have many decorative objects, but on the windowsill in the dining area, there is a glazed jar from the Copenhagen concept store Tadaima and a cast-iron soldier figurine that she found at a flea market years ago. Opposite: The Akari 1N table lamp is by Isamu Noguchi, and the 265 adjustable wall lamp from Flos was designed by Paolo Rizzatto in 1973. The glass vase was a second-hand find.

interior. 'At some point, we'll need to replace all the windows – they're terribly draughty – but we're trying to find someone who can replicate the original style, using the same wood, handles and overall design,' Laura explains. She appreciates the remarkably well-preserved aesthetics of her home, which is a rarity in this affluent neighbourhood.

The interior reflects a thoughtful blend of modern furniture, prototypes of Laura's own designs, vintage finds and a handful of heirlooms. Organic shapes mingle with clean lines, and materials such

as bamboo, bent plywood, wood, steel and natural stone create a harmonious balance. Although the overall look is very clean, almost minimalist, Laura describes herself as a hoarder, albeit one who skilfully keeps things in rotation to ensure her husband and children don't feel overwhelmed by clutter. 'As a designer, I'm drawn to objects that invite interaction and bear traces of a previous life,' she explains. 'I find inspiration in the past and value the opportunity to build on the expertise of those before me. There's no need to spend four months designing a

><

Right: Laura and Mark have no plans to replace the well-preserved tiled bathroom with its blue mosaic floor. Opposite: The couple's bedroom in the basement is furnished with only the essentials: two pine boxes as bedside tables, and two Tolomeo table lamps from Artemide, which were designed by Giancarlo Fassina and Michele De Lucchi in 1987.

chair from scratch if someone else has already perfected the balance of statics, angles and ergonomics.'

This ethos extends to Laura's professional work. Recently, she designed the interior of a coffee shop in central Copenhagen, where the owners wanted to reuse as much as possible. She estimates around 60 per cent of the existing furnishings were repurposed during the refurbishment. Some items were repainted, an old shelving unit was disassembled and rebuilt into new shelves, and the original fluorescent lights were wrapped in sailcloth for a more contemporary aesthetic.

'I'm always mindful of my responsibility to prioritize sustainable thinking in my work,' Laura says. This includes designing furniture to be multifunctional and easy to disassemble, simplifying both transport and eventual disposal. 'For example, our coffee table can be dismantled and converted into a daybed by adding a long cushion I designed. I think it's important to consider whether a product can adapt to a family's changing needs over the years.' She gestures to a daybed in the small TV room, which connects the children's bedrooms and bathroom to the living room and

kitchen. It is one of two daybeds she inherited from her mother, both of which have a lovely history: they were first used by her mother and uncle in their childhood home, and later moved to her grandparents' summer house, where Laura and countless other children slept on them. They are now used by her own children.

'Pieces like this are incredibly valuable to me,' Laura reflects. 'My mother passed away more than ten years ago, and I have so few things from her. The ones I do have, I cherish deeply.'

Curating the Collected

It's hard to imagine that Line Hallberg's grand, second-floor apartment was only ever meant as a temporary home. With its spacious, high-ceilinged rooms, tastefully decorated with light furniture, art and small tableaux, it exudes relaxed elegance and thoughtful aesthetics. Nevertheless, the initial plan was for the family of six to live here only temporarily, as Line and her husband Esben had bought an apartment that was to be renovated from top to bottom. However, obtaining the necessary permits for the renovation

took longer than expected. The project has now lasted eight years, and the family has been living in the rented apartment for two of those years. Line has therefore furnished its 216 square metres (2,325 square feet) with care, ensuring the space feels like a real home. Light and simplicity play a central role here, but there is also room for all the things she and Esben have collected throughout their lives. 'I tend to get attached to some rather silly things, mainly because of their function and the immense craftsmanship that is often behind

✕

This page: Small, charming arrangements of carefully selected finds are placed on windowsills, console tables, pedestals and shelves. Line brought the large seashells and snail shells back home from the Philippines when she worked there 30 years ago. Alongside, the lidded jar is by the contemporary Danish artist Cathrine Raben Davidsen, as is the blue chequered table lamp. The vintage striped vase is from the Danish ceramics workshop Kähler. Opposite: Two vases, also Kähler, are displayed on the 1970s brass and glass shelf unit by Romeo Rega.

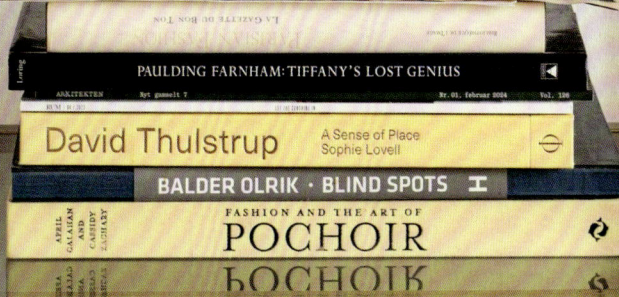

PAULDING FARNHAM: TIFFANY'S LOST GENIUS

ARKITEKTEN   Nyt gammelt T   Nr. 01, februar 2024   Vol. 126

David Thulstrup   A Sense of Place
                         Sophie Lovell

BALDER OLRIK · BLIND SPOTS

FASHION AND THE ART OF
POCHOIR

POCHOIR

⤬

Previous pages and opposite: The light-filled, high-ceilinged dining room is close to being sparsely furnished, with a sculptural concrete dining table by Georg Mengel, dainty chairs by Fratelli Levaggi and a Murano chandelier. The crystal vase is a flea-market find. Against the back wall stands a marble and wrought-iron garden table, serving as a display podium. The large African mask – part of a lighting project Line is working on – is mounted on a lamp stand, still missing a shade. Making a charming addition to the kitchen windowsill are the Tolomeo table lamp from Artemide, two vintage chopping boards and a French church candleholder. Below left: The bamboo stool was designed in the 1960s by Franco Albini. Below right: Line's arrangements make it clear that she selects objects based on form and history.

them,' explains Line, who is a trained goldsmith and runs her own business, Line Hallberg Studio.

Form and aesthetics have always been important in her life – she was born into a family of architects and artists – but she also remembers an experience from her childhood that sparked her interest in foreign cultures, traditions and craftsmanship. 'I had a friend who, at the age of six, went on a round-the-world trip with her parents, something quite unusual back in the late 1970s. When they returned, they had lots of gifts for me, including a Chinese box with leaves that had been dried so only their skeletons remained, and little silk threads were attached to them. It was unbelievably exotic, like unwrapping a piece of world history! Back then, you had to physically travel to get your hands on that kind of thing,' says Line.

Today, her home clearly reflects a fondness for, in particular, Italian design: there's lounge furniture from Gervasoni, dining chairs from Fratelli Levaggi and lamps from Flos and Artemide, not to mention the

many small, elegant vignettes on windowsills, shelves and tables of handcrafted objects and collectables found in flea markets and antique shops in southern Europe. The only Danish pieces in the home are the two concrete coffee and dining tables, created by Georg Mengel, who trained as an engineer and worked in the cement industry before becoming a designer. Line fell in love with them because of the interesting contrast they make with the delicate wooden and rattan chairs. 'I'm very drawn to contrasts, whether it's between the fragile and the sturdy, dark and light, or new and old,' she explains. 'I could never live solely with old furniture; it would feel too overwhelming. That's why our larger pieces are simply chosen for comfort – they shouldn't shout out a particular designer or style.' She adds that it's also deliberate to have only white walls in the home. They serve as a canvas, allowing the stories behind each piece of furniture and object to truly stand out.

Although the larger pieces in the apartment are rarely moved or replaced, Line loves re-experiencing

✕

Previous pages: In the living room, the soft white Ghost armchairs were designed by Paola Navone for Gervasoni. The rice paper lamp from Vitra is the Akari 15A, by Isamu Noguchi. Opposite: Even though the apartment is rented and the kitchen very anonymous, Line has created a cosy dining nook, with a table and bench made by Lars Bjørn of dePlace Furniture. The American Cherner Chairs were designed in 1958 by Norman Cherner, and the picture propped up on the bench is by Jakob Steen. Left: In one corner of the living room, there is an antique French iron stand, which Line either uses in her shop to display jewellery or in her home for hanging green plants.

the joy that the smaller objects have always given her when she repositions them. When she buys something new, it almost always happens during a trip abroad. At home, her senses are already stimulated by working on new jewellery designs, but when she steps outside her familiar surroundings, her eye and curiosity are sharpened in a different way. 'I could never buy something from a website – I'm very sensory and need to see, touch and smell things. On the other hand, I love the chance to wander off in antique shops,' she says. She enjoys finding something completely new but also rediscovering things that have been lingering in the back of her mind, things she might not have been ready for when she first came across them.

Over the years, she has become more interested in the history behind her finds, and she always tries to discover where they come

from, what their function was, how they were made and from which materials. This often leads to direct or indirect inspiration for a new piece of jewellery, but it's not just about creating something new. It's also about understanding and appreciating the deeper layers of history and culture that lie within the objects we find along our way and take with us. 'I believe many people may not fully understand what they're buying, as they tend to focus only on the surface. But when you travel around Italy, for example, you realize that many regions have a long and proud tradition of ceramics and porcelain, and that's why materials, techniques and styles vary so much from place to place.'

✕ TIP

Revamp your space without buying anything new by rearranging the furniture and changing the decor to shift the room's flow and energy. Layer existing textiles, place objects and books in fresh groupings and experiment with swapping rugs and curtains for new textures and colours. A simple yet powerful way to refresh a room is by moving artwork between rooms or rearranging pieces on the walls, giving familiar items a new context. These changes breathe new life into your home, allowing you to rediscover the beauty of what you already own.

Eclectic Seventies

There are few things Nina Marxen loves more than colour, and this is very much in evidence in her 1930s villa. Here, everything, from the walls, ceilings and banisters to the furniture, cushions and picture frames, is adorned with bright and vibrant hues. She plays fearlessly with bold combinations such as pea-green and peach-pink in her home and also in the framing workshop she runs from the basement, which is now a thriving business. Initially trained in management, Nina worked for many years as a consultant, but when she

and her husband Jeffrey had small children and moved to a different part of the country, their daily lives became too difficult to manage, and she longed to see tangible results from her hard work. 'I've always been very interested in art, craftsmanship and everything that involves precision, and one day, when talking to a friend who mentioned her father-in-law had just sold his framing business, something clicked,' she recalls.

At first, Nina was able to set up a workshop in her parents' basement, where she taught herself how to

Above left: Nina likes to fill every corner of her home with art. At the top in a black frame is an etching by Viggo Forting; in the middle a lithograph by Kai Führer; at the bottom an oil pastel painting by Michaela Soldal. Above right: In her daughter's room, she has painted a rippling, dove-blue ribbon around the top of the orange walls, a shade echoed in the woodwork. Opposite: The dining table was bought at auction and lacquered by an auto body shop. Around it are Hans J Wegner's Sawbuck chairs. The lamps are Karlebo, designed by Andreas Hansen for Føg & Morup in the 1960s.

Previous pages and this page: Vintage pine furniture, colourful fabrics, graphic art and decorative glass vases combine to enrich the living room. The blue lithograph above the sofa is by Australian artist Amaina, and the small mirror was found in a second-hand shop. In the hallway, the trio of artworks, from top to bottom, are by Birthe Bindslev, Nina, and Auguste Herbin. Opposite: Pops of orange throughout the living room create a striking contrast with the dove-blue walls. The Nesso table lamp is by Artemide, while the large lithograph is by Richard Mortensen.

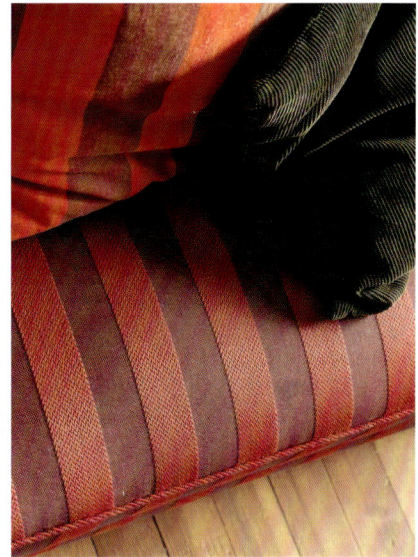

make frames, cut mounts and stretch canvases using YouTube tutorials. After a time, her parents began discussing how their house had become too big for them. Many conversations and deliberations later, Nina managed to persuade Jeffrey that they should buy it – which meant the framing workshop as well.

Apart from a new, custom-built kitchen and a renovation of the dining room – originally a sunroom with a cold slate floor – the most striking transformation is the multitude of colours. Nina recalls how, when she was growing up, the furnishings were primarily white. Though she doesn't believe her love of colours emerged as a form of rebellion, it is remarkable how different the home looks today. 'I have a very '60s–'70s style, and I love orange. I simply can't walk past anything orange without stopping to look at it. If my children had their way, we'd definitely live in a more modern and beige home, but they only have control over their own rooms,' she says with a big grin, while wearing an orange jumpsuit, of course.

The decor in the 194-square-metre (2,088-square-foot) house is vibrant in many ways. The daring colour choices and diverse artworks are counterbalanced by the consistent use of Pomeranian pine floors and an array of wooden furniture, which add warmth and serenity to the space.

Nina often falls for new vintage pieces, and she is forever coming up with ideas about how to enhance their home and bring fresh energy into the rooms. However, Jeffrey has set certain rules to prevent complete chaos and clutter on every shelf and windowsill. 'I'm usually not permitted to buy anything unless I can specify what I'll part with in its place. If I want to rearrange or paint, I'm only allowed to work on one room at a time,' Nina says with a smile. She believes her interior style stands out as distinctive and personal because her tastes are slightly unconventional compared with other people's. This becomes apparent when she's at flea markets or charity shops with friends, and she never reaches for the same items they do. 'I like things that are a bit aggressive, a bit loud, a bit intense. I don't mind if it's right on the edge of what's beautiful,' she reflects.

Most people, even the most devoted thrift enthusiasts, put a limit on what they're willing to buy

Previous pages: A local carpenter, Ludvig Storm, built the kitchen, with birch veneer doors treated with linseed oil and an island made from Oregon pine. The large lithograph is by Ib Geertsen, while Nina made the yellow piece, and the blue work featuring lemons is by Michaela Soldal. The basket hanging on the wall is a gift from a friend who lives in Uganda. Left: Instead of modernizing the bathroom, Nina has used colours and accessories to highlight the vintage yellow tiles. The artwork is by Nina's friend Karen Schmidt (see her home on pages 190–99); the lampshade is an auction find. Opposite: A stunning chrome-oxide green highlights the risers and solid side panel of the staircase. At the top of the stairs is a Bamse Kragh-Jacobsen artwork, which Nina was able to buy cheaply at auction because it was damaged. She repaired it herself.

second-hand. Nina doesn't. She will purchase anything, from bedding and mattresses to cutlery, and her children have learned that it's easier to persuade their mother to buy clothes if they're second-hand. She does admit that certain types of furniture can be harder to find in good condition, but that hardly holds her back. 'I examine upholstered furniture more carefully since it can be dirty and even smelly. The striped sofa had a few stains, but I was so taken by the colour that I couldn't resist bringing it home. It only cost £28, and I figured that if it lasts me two good years, it's better than being discarded,' says Nina, for whom the price has to be just right. That's why she prefers doing her vintage shopping at ordinary charity shops, where she's guaranteed to be the first to spot interesting items – and that usually means she's found a bargain. 'The mere fact that someone's packed it in a box and placed it on a table at a flea market means to me that it's already been discovered, which, of course, makes the treasure hunt much less exciting,' she says.

One thing she's always on the lookout for is old pine picture frames for her workshop, as their quality is far superior to newly produced ones. Unfortunately, the charity shops in her area tend to overprice paintings in frames but, occasionally she convinces them to sell just the frame. 'When you look at the growth rings, you can clearly see the difference in quality between old and new wood. In the old frames, the rings are only a millimetre apart because the trees were allowed to grow more slowly than they are today,' Nina explains.

She then gestures towards the living room, where there are no fewer than four Billy bookcases from IKEA – not the new ones, but the originals designed by Gillis Lundgren in the 1970s. 'When my friend visited, she noticed that the shelves don't sag under the weight of the books – unlike her new ones.'

✕ TIP

Picture frames are expensive these days and are rarely of good quality unless you buy them from a framing workshop. This is why they're best sourced at flea markets and charity shops. Look for simple frames in solid painted or untreated wood. They're usually relatively easy to take apart, allowing you either to sand the frame or paint it in a new colour to suit your artwork. If your artwork has non-standard dimensions, consider hunting for a slightly larger frame and then getting a new mount cut at a glazier's – it will be much cheaper than having a new frame made.

A Symphony of Soft Tones

When Cecilie Bøllingtoft was a child, it wasn't uncommon for her to return home from school to find the living room furniture rearranged or discover a newly refurbished second-hand piece. Her mother had a strong interest in interior design, and today, mother's and daughter's decorating styles are much alike. The three small upholstered sofas that now form the focal point of the living room were, in fact, inspired by an old English sofa from Cecilie's childhood home, which her mother had reupholstered. Reflecting on the sofas, she says:

'It was a deliberate project that took about six months. I found the sofas one at a time and had them reupholstered, even though I hadn't seen the three different patterns together. Fortunately, they worked well, and when we moved, they fitted perfectly into the new living room.'

After a year of hard work, she and her husband Søren have just finished renovating their 240-square-metre (2,583-square-foot) villa. The result is a bright and inviting home, elegant and balanced, where light pastel colours and natural materials play

✕

This page and opposite: Cecilie's home is an eclectic mix of classical and modern elements that come together to create a light and airy feel. The bright green chairs are Carimate by Vico Magistretti, while the sofas were found second-hand and reupholstered. The small rattan footstool is Italian, and the lithograph is by Erik A Frandsen. Overleaf: Custom-built shelves offer a beautiful view through the living rooms. The lounge chairs are CH25 by Hans J Wegner, and the large green table lamp with an opaline glass base and matching green lampshade is a vintage Heiberg piece from Søholm.

Left: In the dining room, David Thulstrup's oak and wicker chairs contrast with the Muller Van Severen dining table, which pairs a lacquered steel frame with a polyethylene top. Originally designed for the celebrated restaurant Noma in Copenhagen, the chairs were later put into production by Brdr. Krüger. The chairs and table were bought new but the room gains character and personality from the antique escritoire and porcelain double candleholder by French designer Jean Roger. Opposite: One of Cecilie's favourite things about the house is the vista through the three adjoining rooms downstairs. Above the double doors in the dining room, plates from the Swedish ceramics manufacturer Rörstrand, dating back to the 1890s, add a sense of history. In the kitchen, a built-in bench brings a modern, rustic feel, while a yellow highchair and a 1970s pendant – both found second-hand – lend warmth and character. The wall-hung plate rack, carefully sanded and repainted, displays Cecilie's collection of finely decorated platters, which echo the William Morris wallpaper in the hallway beyond. A small 1972 lithograph by Henry Heerup complements the wallpaper's colours perfectly.

a central role. The interior brings together new, old, inherited and homemade elements, harmoniously blending with the house's original features from 1934, such as the old doors, frames, stucco ceilings and rosettes, which the couple have made an effort to preserve. 'Before we bought the house, we looked at many others that had been renovated beyond recognition. I think people generally rip out far too many old features and change the layout too

much, which strips away the charm. The most significant change we made was replacing the windows with larger ones to bring more light into the rooms and highlight the fantastic view – and I still think you can sense that it's an old house,' Cecilie explains.

Though their backgrounds in law and political science are far from artistic, the couple clearly have an eye for aesthetics and detail. This is evident in their choice to include porcelain light switches and ceiling-

integrated speakers in their budget, as well as in their use of materials like wood, fabric and glass, to create an intriguing interior that also suits everyday life with two small children. 'One of my core philosophies is that our furniture has to be functional and versatile. That's why we chose a dining table made from a durable material. It's not one I would have specifically sought out, but I fell in love with the design by Muller Van Severen, and luckily it's also very

Opposite and below: Cecilie has kept the large rooms fairly simple in style, allowing the pastel tones of the decoration and the small glass lamps with pleated shades to complement the grand setting. She has been more adventurous in the smaller rooms: the guest toilet is painted a bold raspberry red, while the guest room, featuring a polar bear ozone lamp on the windowsill, is decorated with clover-patterned wallpaper by Josef Frank. Preferring not to use children's plastic furniture, she has opted for second-hand wooden pieces in her daughter's room, including an Alvar Aalto-inspired stool and the extendable Juno cot (crib), which is a family heirloom, designed by Viggo Einfeldt.

practical,' says Cecilie. The wooden dining chairs add a beautiful texture that contrasts with the smooth surface of the table. Designed in 2021 by renowned architect David Thulstrup for the Michelin-starred restaurant Noma, the chairs were bought new, though the couple would have preferred them to be preowned.

Aside from the dining table and chairs, many of the home's furnishings are second-hand finds and some are even scavenged. But they almost always get a new look with a fresh coat of paint or by being reupholstered. Cecilie particularly enjoys buying vintage children's furniture and toys, as she considers them much nicer than the ones available new. 'You can hardly find anything but plastic things for children these days, but there are so many lovely pieces in wood and bamboo.' She often takes her children with her to flea markets, teaching them the joys of shopping second-hand. More frequently, however, she stumbles upon furniture on the street with a 'free' sign. 'I often find wonderful things left out, and just a bit further north, there's a recycling station with a market where everything is free. I love going there. It encourages me to take risks, even if I'm uncertain whether something fits my style because I can always take it back if it doesn't,' Cecilie explains. She adds that she's also rescued old furniture that her neighbour was about to throw out.

She enjoys taking her time to find and restore second-hand pieces when she has a clear vision for them. For instance, she spent several weeks searching for a plate rack that would fit perfectly on the back wall of the kitchen. When she finally found the perfect one, there were so many layers of paint on it that no new paint would

stick. She had to strip off all the layers with a hairdryer before she could start sanding and repainting. 'I definitely spent far too long on it, but the end result was worth every minute,' she says with a laugh.

Cecilie's favourite piece of furniture is the large escritoire at the end of the dining table; she inherited it from her mother, who inherited it from her mother. The dark wood and carved details lend weight and character to the otherwise light decor of the dining room. A friend, who is very interested in history, believes the escritoire was made in the 1820s as a wedding gift. Cecilie is keen to explore the truth behind the theory whenever time allows.

Aside from its sentimental value and intriguing history, the escritoire is important to Cecilie because it's large enough to store all her vintage tablecloths, placemats, napkins, cutlery and glasses – things, she admits, not many women of her age collect. 'My friends tease me for having four different white tablecloths, three different kinds of wine glasses and so on. I'm not really old enough to amass such things, but I love hosting dinner parties and enjoy setting a beautiful table, which makes the occasion feel a little more special.'

✕

Left: Light-coloured surfaces are the perfect backdrop for the dominant artworks in Kristine's large living room. The piece above the daybed is by artist Rie Elise Larsen and is a tribute to the American novelist Zelda Fitzgerald. Opposite: Hans J Wegner's CH07 Shell chair stands alongside one of Kristine's father, Folmer Bendtsen's large oil paintings, depicting a scene in Copenhagen. Overleaf left: Although Arne Jacobsen's Swan lounge chair and Morten Voss's Flightdeck concrete table are from completely different periods, they work well together because of their curved forms and chrome details. Overleaf right: Suspended over the marble-topped Eero Saarinen table is a 1970s mouth-blown glass chandelier from Murano. The brass Liljan candle holder is from Skultuna.

The Artist's Way

When you step into Kristine Bendtsen's 220-square-metre (2,368-square-foot) waterfront villa, her artistic heritage immediately reveals itself: there is art, primarily oil paintings by her father Folmer Bendtsen, adorning every surface. During the 1940s, he gained recognition as the painter of the working class. Throughout his life, he received significant acclaim, including winning the competition to decorate the canteen of Copenhagen's Radiohuset, Vilhelm Lauritzen's architectural masterpiece.

Kristine inherited many of her father's paintings, mostly depictions of working-class life in the urban outskirts, but these didn't resonate with her as much as his earlier works, which include many still lifes and a few portraits. Consequently, she sold much of the collection and instead sought out the pieces that truly spoke to her. 'There's a small work hanging in my hallway, which I've grown really fond of, depicting his brushes, thinner and cleaning spirit. It's such an ordinary scene, but it reminds me of my childhood,' she explains.

Kristine was very creative from an early age, often drawing, collaging or sewing. However, her father encouraged her to pursue a formal education – probably because, as an artist, he knew about the harsh realities and financial struggles that often accompany such a lifestyle. So, she became a dental technician and, for two decades, she crafted lifelike porcelain teeth. Even though she excelled in her field, ten years ago she decided that the rest of her working life should take a different direction. She had always dreamed of having her own business and, with her upbringing in the art world, it was only natural that it would involve art. The lithographs, exhibition posters and original works she sells today, however, differ greatly in expression from the art she grew up with. Yet she finds herself gravitating towards motifs that feel somewhat familiar, even though they don't resemble her father's work in style or colour. 'When I look for art, I can't avoid being influenced by the commercial aspect – it has to be something I can sell. But I think I subconsciously gravitate towards still, calm scenes. There's something about the atmosphere they have, and many of them probably remind me a little of my father's

Above: Thanks to the open floor plan and large windows, nature is always close by, no matter where you are in the house. Kristine acquired the dining table by the Finnish designer Eero Saarinen for American Knoll at a good price – it was a showroom model, and she has a theory that it was hard to sell because the marble tabletop is so dark. The red dining chairs are PP68 by Hans J Wegner, and the sofa is his Airport design. Opposite: Kristine isn't afraid to mix chunky gold frames with simpler frames in silver or painted wood. The large piece in the dining room is by Folmer Bendtsen, her father. The barstool by the kitchen window is Beetle from GUBI.

paintings,' says Kristine, who likes to seek out posters produced in limited editions.

Her gallery is a delightful mix of work by mainly French, Spanish and Italian artists from the first half of the 20th century. Thanks to the special metal rails she inherited from the previous owner of the space, it's easy for her to rotate individual pieces in the display. She sources most of her stock in Paris – both online and in person – where she has many business connections. At the time of purchase, she usually already has a clear idea of how a frame should look, what colour it should be, and whether it requires a mount or background. Kristine paints and gilds the frames herself, a task completed in her and her husband Peter's home, a 30-minute drive from the gallery. Here, the atmosphere is much calmer, given that it is not an exhibition space for customers. The couple bought and renovated the villa in 2013, establishing an open-plan layout with large windows, which creates a wonderful connection to the salt marsh and sea that lie just beyond the garden gate.

The decor of the airy, light-filled rooms is modern, elegant and functional, with a clear balance

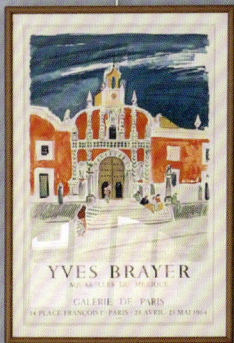

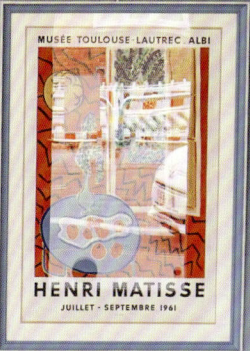

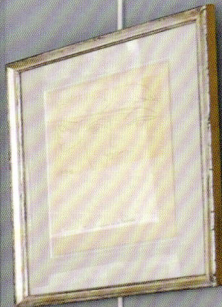

✕

Previous pages, left and below: In her gallery, Kristine uses the original metal rails to display a dynamic mix of primarily French posters, with both abstract and figurative motifs complementing each other in colour and expression. The low footstool at the far right is the Doughnut stool and was designed by Rud Thygesen and Johnny Sørensen for Magnus Olesen in 1974. Most of the other pieces of furniture in the gallery are vintage or made by Kristine's son, who has a carpentry workshop. Artist Pylle Søndergaard designed the owl vases. Opposite: In the entrance to the couple's home, a streamlined stool designed by Antonio Citterio for Flexform in the 1990s is paired with a plaster bust and one of Folmer Bendtsen's oil paintings.

between artistic expression and comfort. The pieces of furniture are almost exclusively auction purchases – the couple live just minutes away from a local auction house that brings in many Danish and international pieces, making the hunting process both convenient and hassle-free for her. 'I like being able to pop over and look at something specific, go home, go online, place a bid and know exactly what I'm bidding on. I'm probably a bit cautious about buying things unseen, so it's a huge advantage that I can inspect items in person,'

Kristine says. This doesn't mean she shies away from buying a fixer-upper. Provided she knows what she's getting into and the price reflects the condition of the piece, she's willing to take a chance. For instance, six years ago, she purchased a severely damaged example of Arne Jacobsen's classic Swan Chair, which had lost all its foam and shed dust when sat on. Nonetheless, she used it for five years, simply spraying a little fabric glue into it whenever it started to shed, before finally having it restored and reupholstered a year ago. 'It was still

This page: Kristine hangs some of the surplus works from the gallery in the main guest room. Opposite: The original conservatory, converted into a second guest room, also serves as an exhibition space for some of her plaster figures and busts. The floor lamp is from Artemide, the table lamp from Warm Nordic. Part of Kristine's sculpture collection is arranged on the pink Montana chest of drawers. The table lamp, oil painting and Tolomeo wall lamp by Artemide complement the room's colours. A wood-framed mirror, made by Kristine's son, and a platter by Pylle Søndergaard decorate the bathroom walls.

beautiful when viewed from the back, and I could easily see the potential. But no one else was allowed to sit in it,' Kristine recalls with a smile.

She considers herself very impulsive, rarely planning new purchases and instead acting only when something speaks to her. These days, she finds herself buying much less, having reached a point where she feels the decoration of her home is complete – unless, of course, she comes across an intriguing work of art by her father. Sometimes, friends and acquaintances tip her off when they spot such an artwork for sale, but last summer, she literally stumbled upon one. 'I had parked in front of the auction house and was walking across the car park when I passed an older lady struggling with a large painting in her car. I stopped, and it turned out to be the most amazing piece by my father. We had a long chat about how incredibly coincidental it was, and I placed a bid on it, but it ended up going for a price that was far too high. Others had also recognized its value.'

✕TIP

The frame can have a significant impact on how an artwork is perceived. A new and different frame can revitalize a piece, add depth and cohesion and make it more suitable for a contemporary home. It may be helpful to consult an experienced framer to ensure that the artwork's expression, level of detail, colour tones and size, and the room where it will be displayed, are all carefully considered.

Playful Contrasts

Peter Andersen and Karin Winther's 197-year-old farmhouse doesn't offer much ceiling height or elbow room – just 66 square metres (710 square feet) on the ground floor and barely 40 (430) upstairs. However, what it lacks in space, it more than makes up for in charm and character. This is apparent the moment you step into the hallway and kitchen, where a low doorframe prompts you to duck your head. Peter, a musician, and Karin, a graphic designer, have lived here for almost six years, though one could

easily believe they've been here for decades. Few homes are as full of life and personality, and replicating their decor style would be a challenge because it's so uniquely curated. Design classics such as the Eames DSR dining chair, Poul Kjærholm's PK22 lounge chair and Arne Jacobsen's Swan chair are paired with exhibition posters, lithographs and drawings by European artists, as well as French church candelabras, plaster sculptures and plastic figurines. All the items have been painstakingly

collected over a lifetime, making it through divorces, life crises, moving home – and a partner who doesn't always share exactly the same taste. 'If I lived alone, I'd probably decorate more cartoonishly,' says Peter with a smile. 'I'm very drawn to the comic book worlds, especially Tintin, and I've always admired artists like Andy Warhol and Roy Lichtenstein who embraced that crash-bam-pow style. When we were kids, my siblings and I weren't allowed to read Donald Duck comics because our parents viewed

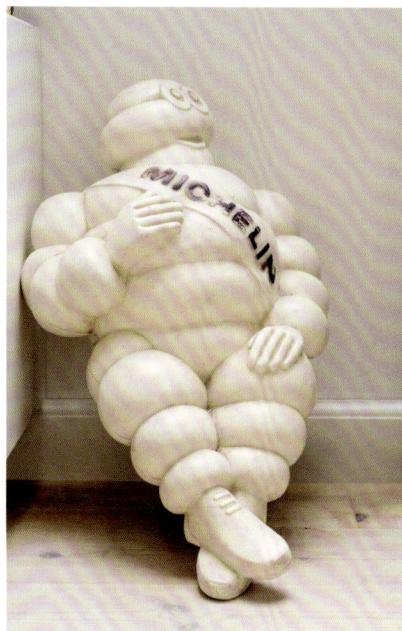

Far left: The small, cosy kitchen was in the house when Peter and Karin took it over, but they have painted it and added shelves. Left: Peter has a particular fondness for Michelin Men, especially if they serve a function, like this lamp. Opposite: There is a relaxed and informal atmosphere in the light country house. The lounge chairs are by Poul Kjærholm, and the vintage table lamps are from Kaiser Idell. An old decorative letter hangs on the wall by the stairs. Overleaf: Around the rustic dining table are new and old Eames DSR chairs in fibreglass and plastic. Peter inherited the two smaller lithographs by Karel Appel, while the large one by Pierre Alechinsky was purchased at Galerie Maeght in Paris.

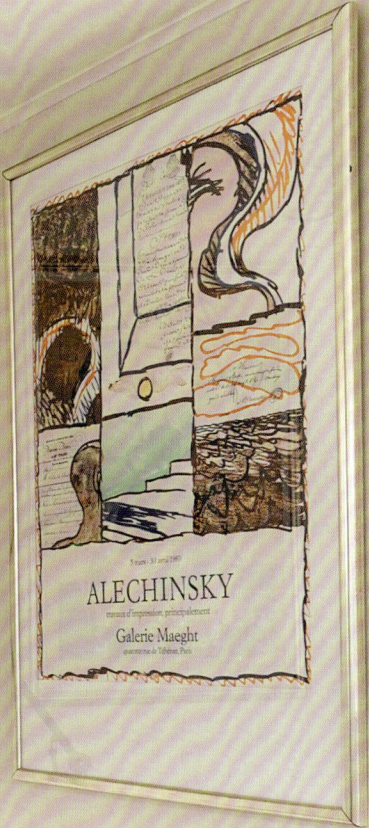

Left: Even though space is tight in the hallway, the couple have incorporated a small bench with a lantern, a vase and a vintage exhibition poster to ensure it doesn't feel overly practical. Opposite: Peter and Karin work extensively with lighting in their interior design and are generally of the belief that having more light sources is preferable to having too few – that way, you can always turn off the ones you don't need. A Louis Poulsen PH Artichoke lamp, also known as 'The Cone' due to its pinecone-like shape, hangs in one corner of the living room. Designed in 1958 by Poul Henningsen, it's an heirloom from Karin's mother.

them as imperialistic, corrupting literature from the US. But one day, my godfather, a renowned professor of Roman history, came by with a stack of Asterix comics, and my mother couldn't say no.'

Having grown up in a home where there was a strong appreciation for art and design, Peter takes the lead on choices for the interior and has contributed most of the items in the couple's home. However, Karin usually has an opinion on what crosses the threshold, often steering the style in a slightly more minimal direction. She's also the one to voice concerns if things become too cluttered, and she isn't afraid to veto certain items. For instance, she's banned Peter's porcelain café-logo ashtrays from the house. He loves their graphic design, especially the large red and blue ones for the Italian vermouth Cinzano, but Karin feels they give the wrong impression – particularly to Peter's grandchildren, who often visit – so they've been relegated to the garden. On the other hand, she has no objections to the plaster sculptures and 1960s

Right: To stop books cluttering up the small living rooms, the couple make use of all the wall space, including over the stairs, where Peter's collection of alarm clocks is also displayed. Below: The brass and coloured glass candlestick on the living room windowsill originally came from a French church. Opposite: The annex has been turned into a B & B. Home to a tower of paperbacks, with lithographs alongside, the dining room is furnished with J46 spindle chairs by Poul M Volther for FDB Mobler and a bench. A vintage workshop lamp hangs over the table.

drawings of nude or lightly clothed women in Peter's collection. 'I treasure the sculptures because they exude a liberated energy in the way they lift their chests and hold their hair up. Their expressions reveal a self-assured sexuality, which was bold and powerful for their time,' she explains.

As a teenager, Peter began visiting flea markets. He developed an interest in items with age and history, inspired by some older friends who had opened a vintage shop. Before turning 18, he made his first major purchase: an old hot dog cart with wooden wheels and a basin inside. 'It eventually fell apart, but I used it as a bar at a few parties. Back in the early '80s, there were no digital platforms and almost no shops, so you could only find things at flea markets,' Peter recalls. At one point, his family bought a summer house on an island at the other end of the country, where a man sold quirky old advertising signs. Peter purchased a few, including an almost 2-metre (6½-ft) tall Nivea sign featuring a woman in a white swimsuit. Unfortunately, it was stolen, along with many other cherished finds, when someone broke into the attic where he stored many of his items, but he still remembers the sign vividly. Today, there aren't many advertising signs left in his collection, but a single enamel one from Danish chewing-gum maker Stimorol has decorative value in the upstairs TV room, where there are also two plastic Michelin Men – a character Peter has always adored. His favourite find, however, is an Italian opaline glass pendant hanging in the bedroom. 'I found it at a flea market in Draguignan, a

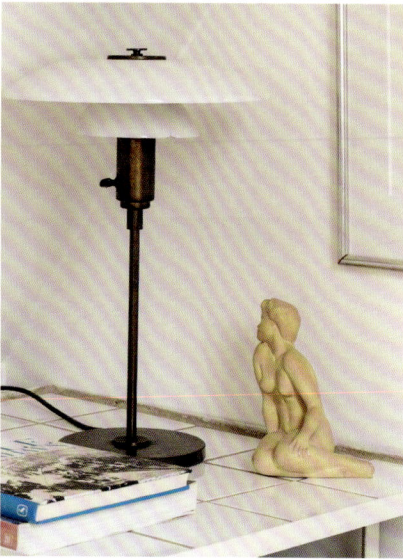

✕

Left and opposite above: The TV room in the eaves is furnished with light textiles, green plants, woven baskets and small collectables in the form of metal tins, plaster figures and enamel signs. Karin bought the Swan chair by Arne Jacobsen at auction many years ago. Covering the cracked leather seat with a sheepskin has made it suitable for sitting on and extended the chair's life. Opposite below: The large Jean Dubuffet lithograph over the bed is from 1960. The bathroom remains much as it did when the couple moved in, but Peter has added his own touch with plaster sculptures and a slightly cheeky drawing.

town in southern France, and it holds special meaning for me, not only because of the cartoon-like pattern but also because it survived the car journey home,' he says.

Over the past four decades, Peter has refined his taste and extended his knowledge of art, design and antiques so much so that he can confidently select items that have both aesthetic and historical value. His collection has become a reflection of this deeper understanding. Although

he hardly buys any vintage pieces these days, he keeps an eye out for them, even in places where nothing seems to be for sale – such as in friends' homes. Occasionally, he's had luck persuading people to sell him something, as a friend recalls: 'He was as bold as brass, and if he drove by a house and could see something interesting through the window, he'd pull over and knock on the door. Typically, he would be told that what he'd seen wasn't for sale,

but that could change once a price was mentioned,' he says with a grin.

The most important thing for Peter about a vintage piece isn't the name of the designer or artist, but that it is genuinely as old as it appears. In recent decades, a large market has emerged for things that look old and worn but are, in fact, newly produced, something that Peter always steers clear of. 'It's important to me that a piece is authentic. It always has been. If it's not the real deal, I don't want it.'

✕ TIP

When selecting vintage items for your home, opt for pieces crafted from warm, natural materials such as wood, bamboo, rattan and leather. They not only bring texture and warmth to a space but also have an inherent timelessness that complements a variety of interior styles. Rattan and bamboo, often found in vintage furniture, offer a lightness and airiness that work especially well in spaces with a modern or minimalist feel, while still providing a subtle connection to the past.

✕

Left: Karen loves buying art and mixing graphics, fabric prints, paintings and photographs in a cross-disciplinary way. Placing glass in a former doorway to the dining room has brightened the previously dark corridor, allowing the artwork to be appreciated. Opposite: Vintage copper moulds at the entrance to the dining room meet new IKEA cabinets, while Egon Eiermann SE68 orchestra chairs from 1951 meet the Skovby pine dining table from the 1970s. Hanging over the table are two pendant lights by Poul Henningsen. The picture above the right-hand cabinet is by Michaela Soldal; those on the left were found at flea markets.

The House on the Hill

As it stands on the hilltop, with its rendered exterior and pointed roof, towering over numerous single-storey, yellow-brick houses, Karen Schmidt's villa appears quite odd. Built in 1931 on a vast plot of land, the villa's owner was a man who enjoyed gambling. When he had accrued significant gambling debts, he sold off portions of his property. Inevitably, the smaller houses then built on the land below were close together. Even so, the villa still has over 1,200 square metres (12,917 square feet) of garden, offering ample space for growing flowers and vegetables, as well as for relaxing or gathering around the outdoor dining table while enjoying the view of the neighbourhood.

After buying the house, Karen and her husband Kasper waited four years to begin the renovation project due to its scale and cost; they even sold their summer house to help fund it. Fortunately, the outcome has been exactly as they envisioned. The house now includes all the modern conveniences a family could wish for, yet every element appears as though it has always been a part of the home. 'It was essential for me that the house retained its character and didn't end up looking like a new build, so we preserved as many old details as we could manage. For example, there were four different flooring materials used on the ground level. We chose to keep just the floorboards, even though they were, in places, completely perforated by woodworm,' Karen explains. Along the way, they also discovered a mosaic ceiling, typically found in gaming halls, in the kitchen. Unfortunately, it was in very poor condition, but it

Right: There's hardly a square metre (yard) in Karen's home without a piece of art in some form or other. Most pictures have been reframed, to suit the overall feel of the space. In the vertical line of artworks in the dining room, the photographic work at the top is by Trine Søndergaard, the graphic image in the middle by Cecilia de Jong, and the print at the bottom by John Anderskow. Opposite: With its open cabinets, the bespoke kitchen offers a great opportunity to showcase personality through cups, glasses, bowls and vases. Another trio, this time of plates, hangs by the kitchen window. The top one was produced in the Polish faience factory Włocławek in the 1970s; the middle one is Spanish, from the 1960s; the bottom one is from the porcelain factory Lise Porcelæn, which created a series of plates featuring Danish folk costumes in the 1980s. It is an heirloom from Kasper's family, who are from the island of Fanø. According to family lore, the woman on the plate is his grandmother. Behind the houseplant, the large lithograph by Frede Troelsen was found at auction, while the watercolour below is by Henrik Marxen. In the conservatory, lightweight bamboo garden furniture, all of it second-hand, together with summery textiles and string lights create a relaxed and intimate space.

remains in place under the plaster ceiling as a quiet, unseen testament to the house's fascinating history.

One of the reasons the couple chose this particular house was that the basement, which had been used to print illegal papers for the Danish resistance movement during the Second World War, had already been converted into a pottery workshop by the previous owner. At that time, Karen dreamed of making ceramics full-time, and for four years she lived out that dream as a self-employed potter. However, as the renovation

progressed, it became obvious that it was too financially challenging to continue, so today she manages a department at DSB, Denmark's national railway company, while pursuing ceramics as a hobby.

Through her work with clay and glazes, Karen has developed a keen sense of form and colour. This is particularly evident on the upper floors of the villa, where each room is painted in its own distinctive colour, and the furniture – a mix of old and new – has been well chosen to create balance and contrast.

That one could buy furniture and accessories second-hand wasn't something Karen as a young woman considered doing. It simply never occurred to her. But when the couple bought a summer house in an area known for its many excellent flea markets and thrift shops, a new world unfolded for her, fostering a blossoming passion for discovering preloved treasures. 'It became a shared passion for us, and my husband has even started a side business alongside his full-time job, where he sources, refurbishes

GALERIE
MAEGHT
PALAZUELO
EUROPÆERNE
COLOUR IN ART
LIBERTY
VERDENSKUNSTEN
DANSK KUNST

and resells used lamps, shipping to customers around the world,' she explains. Today, she would never think of buying anything new without first checking its availability as a preowned option.

Karen primarily finds inspiration for her interior design in English home magazines, where she picks up keywords about style periods or countries of origin. She then uses them to search for similar items on platforms like Etsy, whose extensive collection can otherwise feel overwhelming. For example, she might come across a beautiful plate described as Transylvanian and from the 1970s, giving her something to pursue. 'I mostly buy small items on Etsy, but I also have my eye on two Art Nouveau armchairs from former Czechoslovakia. They are a bit too expensive for my budget, but I would snag them if I could. For me, second-hand doesn't have to be cheap – I'm happy to pay the same for an old sofa as a new one would cost, as long as the quality and condition are right,' she says. However, on a few occasions she has ordered items for the home

Previous pages and left: Karen has chosen to paint the darkest of the two living rooms emerald-green. She knew the colour wouldn't exactly brighten up the space, but she dreamed of creating a cosy, embracing feel. The decor here is a little heavier, more upholstered and a little more old-fashioned than in the other rooms. All the furniture and decorative objects were found second-hand. The pearl-encrusted cushion with lobsters is from Studio Hafnia, and the blue cushion with citrus fruits from Svenskt Tenn. The graphic blue artwork is by Nina Marxen, while the small orange one is by Michaela Soldal. Opposite: Sitting on the traditional barley-twist side table is a sunflower table lamp. Karen's parents bought it in Tuscany during one of her childhood holidays but they never truly warmed to it. So when her mother moved house, Karen was delighted to inherit it.

✕

Opposite: Romantic details such as the mirror with its woven frame and painted porcelain lamps and candlesticks have helped to create a warm feel in both the bedroom and the wet room. The slender vase on the bedroom windowsill is a vintage Kähler piece, while the floral plate on the adjacent wall is from the Swedish porcelain factory Rörstrand. Karen bought the small wooden stool in the wet room on Instagram. The sink, sanitaryware and shower fixtures are from Aquadomo.

that turned out to be in worse condition than expected or simply the wrong size. 'Once I bought some lovely wall plates online, but when they arrived, they were tiny,' she says with a laugh, adding that it is often her nostalgic soul that gets the final say. For instance, while many would find it silly to hang antique pudding moulds on the walls in a brand-new kitchen, she loves the contrast. They remind her of old Swedish and English farmhouses, full of character, with brick fireplaces and copper pans on the walls. As she admits, 'There's definitely a part of me that would have liked to live in another time.'

In addition to Facebook Marketplace and Etsy, she frequently explores Instagram for curated second-hand items, where the selection is often more thoughtfully presented but tends to be pricier. However, one can usually request

specific items or ask sellers to keep an eye out for them while on their buying trips – something Karen often takes advantage of. She always trusts her intuition when it comes to decorating, preferring not to create mood boards, colour schemes or plans for hanging art. After all, she can simply take the pictures down and repaint if needed. (Fortunately, Kasper is supportive of her ever-evolving ideas and happily takes the kids to the playground, giving her the peace she needs whenever she's repainting a room.) 'I like that the decoration isn't overly considered, and I don't mind at all if something has a chip or a scratch. I never alter the things I buy either; they go straight into my home. I do think that more permanent features like ceilings and tiles should be well thought out beforehand. But furniture, fabric and so on are easier to play around with and change.'

✕ TIP

When hanging artworks, try varying the spacing and height of each piece slightly for a relaxed, uncoordinated look. Avoid aligning everything too precisely. Instead, let some pieces sit slightly off-centre or at staggered heights. Mixing frame styles and sizes can also help break up any overly structured feel, giving the wall a more organic, collected-over-time look. For extra flexibility, consider leaning a few pieces on shelves or against a wall, so not everything is fixed in place.

At the Picture-Framer's

From the outside, the charcoal-grey farmhouse, built in 1880, looks fairly modest, but once you step over the threshold, it feels entirely different. Although the ceilings aren't particularly high, the rooms feel bright and airy, perhaps due to all the mirrors and reflective glass from the many framed artworks. Everywhere, small, decorative arrangements catch the eye, but there's just enough space between the ornaments for the look not to feel cluttered. For more than 20 years,

Cathrine Boye and her husband Niels have made this house their home. Before moving in, they had lived in various places, including abroad, but when their first child was born, they began searching for a house. 'By pure chance, we passed by this farmhouse and saw that someone was in the middle of a viewing, so we knocked on the door. The house was very old and worn, but there was a pear tree in the garden where we could hang a swing, and that was what we'd dreamed of,' she explains. It was originally

known as The Poplar House, after the poplar trees that once stood in the garden. At one time, it was a café and a restaurant, as evidenced by a huge wooden sign in the kitchen. Cathrine and her husband found the sign in the attic, and while digging in the garden they also came across old cream jugs, beer bottle caps and other relics revealing the house's fascinating past as a guesthouse.

Since taking over the house in 1997, they have expanded the floor plan, building an extension in the

Left: Wooden folding rulers with brass fittings, stored in a preserving jar, add a decorative touch to Cathrine's worktable. Far left: Upstairs, beautifully framed works are stacked, waiting to be moved to new homes. Opposite: Six black-lacquered Y-chairs by Hans J Wegner surround the rustic pine dining table, decorated with glass tealight holders and a Lebrillo, a painted ceramic bowl from the Fajalauza factory in Granada. A 1920s Danish *ampel* chandelier hangs over the table. Overleaf: There is a lovely view into the dining room from the kitchen. The Provençal pickling jars are used for herbs and flowers from the garden.

STEINBERG

Above left: There are many small, carefully arranged displays in the couple's home. The simple vignette on the table includes old wedding goblets and a glass candlestick, with a vintage lithographic poster by Tàpies on the wall behind. Above right: Niels suggested the soft pink colour for the new linen sofa – he thought white would be too dull. The coffee table is from Skovshoved Møbelfabrik, the lounge chair is by Poul Kjærholm, and the Bestlite floor lamp, designed by Robert Dudley Best, is from GUBI. Cathrine was finally able to buy the small wooden horse sculpture from a Swedish antiques dealer after pestering him for months to find one for her. Opposite: The many earthenware pots, bowls, chopping boards and store signs give the kitchen a Mediterranean feel.

same style but with vaulted ceilings, creating a wonderful sense of space. They've also installed a classic kitchen, which, despite being 16 years old, still looks beautiful. Cathrine dreams of tearing down an old shed in the backyard in the next few years, and building a new one that will function as a workshop and storage space. She has largely had free rein with the interior design of the house, as Niels, in her words, is 'the sweetest and most tolerant person in the world', putting up with all her quirky ideas. 'He doesn't quite understand my weakness for wooden decoy ducks, and I think he believes we have enough of them. But the thing is, you can never have too many,' Cathrine adds with a smile.

She's actually a schoolteacher, specializing in Danish, French and arts and crafts, but for the past two years, she's spent more and more time

restoring antique wooden frames and selling them through her Instagram profile, which bears her name. What started as a small hobby during the pandemic has grown into a business, and now she splits her time evenly between the local primary school and her workshop on the first floor of the house. 'I've always been interested in old silver frames, but they've become quite expensive, and many of those you find are in poor condition and rotting. So, I began silvering frames for myself,' she explains. At one point, a friend asked if she could make a frame for her, and word soon spread among her circle of friends. One day, Cathrine was contacted by the owner of a large interiors shop who wanted to buy 20 framed pictures at once. She began by buying just one pack of silver for herself, but before she knew it, she was silvering for hours every day. Now, she orders 250 packs at a

✕

This page: With doors that open out onto the garden, the bright living area is furnished with a Swedish folding table and Thonet chairs. A bronze vase by Tage Andersen and a Bestlite table lamp sit on the table. Cathrine found all the artworks on the walls herself, mostly in France, and framed them in her small workshop on the first floor. Her parents brought back the large olive jar from Mallorca when package holidays (vacation packages) began in the 1970s. Her mother, who has since passed away, purchased an extra seat for the flight back just so she could bring it home.

time. Over the last few years, as her business has grown, the house has also served as a showroom where customers can come, by appointment, to view the artworks she has for sale. This is why there are always plenty of fresh flowers in the vases, and – in principle – everything on the walls is for sale. However, there are a few things she won't part with, but as she says with a laugh, 'I think I'd have to pack more than a suitcase if the house were on fire.'

Art has always played a significant role in Cathrine's life. She comes from an artistic family and, as an art teacher, she is deeply interested in form and colour theory and has extensive knowledge of art history. 'I love reading about the lives of the artists. I also think it adds value to a picture when you know that, for example, this is actually Picasso's first wife, Olga, and that she was a Bolshoi ballerina. It's fun to know what's hanging on the wall,' she explains. And it's not just the artwork that must have a story – even the vases, candlesticks and sculptures clearly had another life before finding their place in the farmhouse. Her collection includes earthenware jars from France, wooden toys

from Sweden and Chinese burial figurines. It's important to Cathrine that these items originally served a clear function and weren't merely decorative pieces. She calls herself a collector and often reads auction catalogues to learn more about the origins of the various things she acquires – for example, the small, pastel-coloured opaline glass boxes, from the 19th century, were also known as sugar boxes, because they were used by the ladies of the house to hide sugar cubes from the servants.

Some of the highlights of the year are her regular trips to France, which are scheduled around the markets in different towns. Her daughter is often invited along to help carry purchases, and they each take two bags with them – one full and one empty. 'There are strict orders not to overpack, because you can wear the same clothes for two days, so there's room

for all the things we find,' she says. She then adds that it's not as though the French markets are overflowing with treasures waiting to be plucked off the shelves – they have their fair share of less desirable items, just like markets anywhere else.

While most of the interior is sourced second-hand, more modern pieces, such as a sofa, lounge chair and table lamp, are also thoughtfully placed. These items don't overshadow the carefully selected antiques but they do prevent the home from feeling like a museum. 'I know that I need to be careful not to make it too old-fashioned. I just find that many new items have a rather harsh look – it's something about the shapes and the smooth surfaces,' says Cathrine. 'I love the tactile quality of a beautiful glaze that's slightly run, and I really don't mind that my dish from Alsace has been mended.'

Above left and right: The bedroom is located in an extension, designed to complement the style of the house. Cathrine's assured use of colour and attention to detail are evident here too. A 19th-century Louis Philippe mirror and a 1950s table lamp, made by the French ceramicist Gustave Reynaud, stand on the vintage bureau. The woollen rug is from Kusiner Carpets. Opposite: According to Cathrine, one can never have too many wooden decoy ducks, antique Swedish mirrors or opaline boxes. The boxes are expensive these days, so she only allows herself one per year.

✗ TIP

Second-hand mirrors often have a charm and character that new mirrors simply lack. Depending on your style, you can opt for organically shaped mirrors with wooden frames, antique ones with silvered or gilded carved frames, or perhaps a Venetian mirror with beautiful facet cuttings and decorations. Use full-length mirrors in the bedroom or hallway, and smaller mirrors above the sink in the bathroom and in the living room, to make the space appear larger and brighter. Be mindful that old mirrors may suffer from mirror rot, oxidation or other forms of discoloration, which makes them less practical for certain things, such as using as a makeup mirror.

Hunting for the Handmade

As you turn onto the gravel road leading to the old folding ruler factory, there's very little to suggest that you're about to discover a treasure-trove of vintage furniture, lamps and handcrafted curiosities. The two-storey, red-brick building doesn't draw much attention to itself, and there are no big signs telling you what's inside. But should you step through the door, you'll be greeted by two friendly young men who, with genuine enthusiasm, will guide you through their showroom, sharing the stories behind their exceptional collection.

'We had a few crazy years at the start,' explains Elias Hjorth Ingstrup, one half of eliaselias, the vintage shop that he runs with his business partner Benjamin Elias Johansen. 'We'd drive around buying stock, put it up for sale and then deliver the goods, often with 10 to 12 stops per trip. Wanting to give our customers a little extra, we'd also help carry heavy furniture into their homes. Our days started early in the morning and ended between ten and midnight.' While Elias has a good eye for the more classic pieces, Benjamin has a knack for spotting furniture

and objects that might not seem immediately marketable but could attract a great deal of interest in the right context. Handmade is a key word for both of them and one of the cornerstones behind the success of eliaselias.

Once the COVID-19 pandemic had ended and people were again able to travel, interest in furniture and interior design declined – a shift that everyone in the industry experienced – and items that once had five potential buyers sometimes struggled to attract even one. As a result, the two

Left and opposite: The shelves in the eliaselias showroom are a treasure-trove for vintage enthusiasts. Danish and Swedish bowls, stools and figures in light and dark wood stand side by side, waiting for a new home. In one corner, a 1960s bamboo lounge chair from Italy is paired with a three-legged pine stool and wooden hat blocks resembling minimalist sculptures. The Swedish, U-shaped pine stool from the 1950s is a perfect example of wabi-sabi, an aesthetic that finds beauty in nature's imperfections. The hand-carved oak dining chair, also Swedish, likely dates back to the early 1900s.

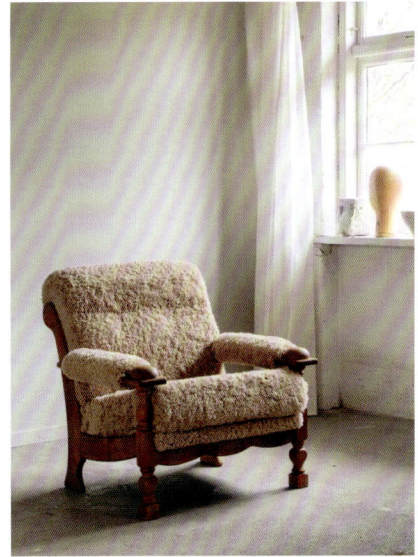

✕

Previous pages: The focus of the two treasure hunters isn't so much on names and periods as it is on interesting forms. In their warehouse, you can find everything from Rainer Daumiller's 1970s brutalist chairs to intricately carved chests and cupboards dating back to the rococo. Opposite: Broad-backed dining chairs, model 3245, by Børge Mogensen surround the pine table of unknown provenance. Hans-Agne Jakobsson designed the ceiling light; Ole Victor, Elias's father, created the floor vase and painting. Above left and overleaf: A warm and inviting retreat, the old farmhouse has a view of the forest that can be enjoyed from the Maralunga sofa, designed by Vico Magistretti for Cassina in 1973. The marble-topped, wooden coffee table was a second-hand find. While the legs are technically meant to face the other way, Elias prefers this arrangement, as it makes the table slightly lower. The hand-carved Nigerian Nupe stool with pointed legs dates back to the early 20th century. Above right: Henning Kjærnulf designed the solid oak, bouclé armchair.

vintage hunters decided to shift their sales strategy from primarily selling to Copenhageners on Instagram to selling almost exclusively to the United States, where the typical customer is an interior designer or stylist with very specific preferences. Today, they can pack and ship even large pieces of furniture, and they've hired their own upholsterer to ensure that the old stools, armchairs and sofas they find are restored to their former glory and ready for a new life across the Atlantic. And the business is thriving, so much so that it will soon be moving to new, larger premises, for which they have ambitious plans: 'We don't just want to run a vintage shop; we want it to be the place where companies come to have the coolest photoshoots. We'd also like to start building some small cabins that we can place in various locations, which people can rent and enjoy the same experience with curated furniture and art,' says Elias.

When the two young men started their business, they were among the very first in the industry to buy pine furniture in large quantities, and many of their colleagues exchanged puzzled looks, calling them 'The Pine

Boys'. At that time, pine had been out of fashion for decades, especially the lacquered kind, as it was often associated with nurseries, schools and summer houses – places where it was commonly used due to its low cost and durability. 'We both appreciate the texture, warmth and distinctive grain of pine, so we purchased it out of love, not with the expectation that it would become trendy again. However, we're now noticing that others are beginning to sell it too, driven by demand, especially in the US, Japan and China,' explains Elias.

Since starting the business, Elias has married and had a son, and the family of three live in a charming 1918 farmhouse, which once belonged to a nearby estate but now stands completely isolated in a picturesque woodland setting. Originally, the house was much smaller, but previous owners extended it and opened up the upstairs floor, which they now use as an office and TV room. Among other improvements, the couple installed large windows facing the beautiful, secluded garden, which transitions into the surrounding forest. They also have plans to build a new kitchen, albeit on a budget.

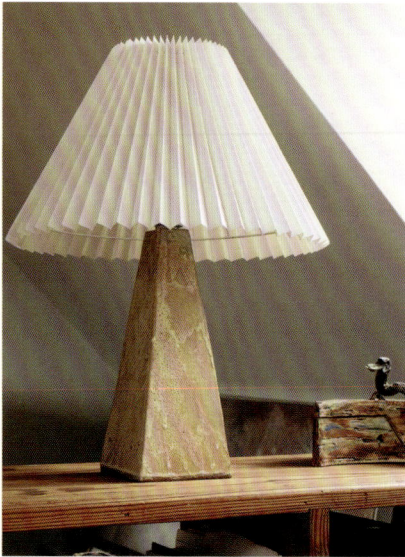

✖

Left: Ole Victor crafted the ceramic table lamp. Opposite: Elias, who works with pine for his work, also incorporates it into his home. Upstairs, he's set up a small office with a 1940s desk attributed to Philip Arctander, complemented by a zigzag chair from the 1980s and a ceiling light by Hans-Agne Jakobsson. To the right of the doorway is a Swedish stump chair, carved from a single log, while to the left stands a floor lamp made from an old organ pipe. Elias displays his collection of decorative cups, plates and bowls in a vintage pine shelving unit. The bedside lamps are by Jan Wickelgren, and the relief wall sculpture is by Gunnar Kanevad.

Walking through the rooms, it's clear that Elias's work influences the look of his home. Many of the pieces were initially bought for the business but found their way home with him because he fell in love with them. The space showcases both classic design pieces and several handcrafted works by carpenters – many, of course, in pine. The golden glow of the wood, combined with the muted wall colours and rugs on the floors, creates a warm, enveloping atmosphere, almost like a hug. Despite being constantly exposed to new vintage pieces, Elias is quite attached to the furniture and objects that surround him, which is why nothing much changes in his home.

The same can't be said about the stock, though, where new treasures are continually making their way into the old factory and out to discerning customers, fostering a continuous movement in the inventory. Here, one can encounter a range of styles – from elegant antique and intricate art deco to sleek mid-century modern and raw brutalism, alongside a wealth of artisanal crafts that are difficult to date. The duo primarily source their pieces from various corners of Europe, and although they typically embark on their journeys with a specific destination in mind, they are known to take delightful detours should something intriguing catch their eye. For instance, during a recent buying trip to Sweden, they happened to pass by some old barns where they discovered an antique dealer they had yet to visit. 'When we initially started dealing in vintage items, we often visited foreign markets to sell, but now we travel as buyers,' Elias explains, eagerly anticipating the day when his son is old enough to accompany him on these excursions. However, the true joy of being away lies not in the finds themselves but in the immense knowledge gained from colleagues in France, Belgium, Italy and Sweden. 'In Denmark, I believe we've tended to focus a bit too much on Danish classics. Southern European dealers, in particular, are brilliant at mixing different styles from various periods. There are virtually limitless possibilities for how you can decorate, if you dare to.'

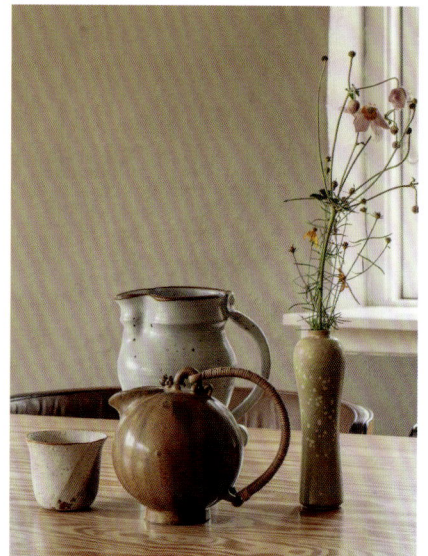

✖TIP

Make sure that the items you buy suit your (and possibly your family's) everyday life. If you have young children, it's probably best to avoid light bouclé upholstery and delicate ceramics, and if you dislike handwashing, steer clear of vintage crystal glasses, butter knives with bone handles and other such items that can't go in the dishwasher.

Acknowledgements

Writing a book about vintage has been a dream of mine for many years, and I am incredibly grateful that it has finally come to fruition. A huge thank you to my publisher, Alison Starling, for believing in me from the very beginning, and for allowing me to bring my vision to life without compromise. And a heartfelt thanks to the entire team at Octopus for their patience with a rather demanding and perfectionist author!

The process of creating this book has been fun, inspiring, and thought-provoking. As you will have read in the opening pages, I have my own reasons for avoiding new purchases, but I had no idea there were so many different ways into the world of vintage. It has only reinforced my belief that there is no single type of person who buys vintage, and no one particular way that a home furnished with vintage pieces should look. Vintage is, quite simply, for everyone, and it is not just about aesthetics – it is about making conscious choices, not only in how we decorate our homes but in how we live our lives.

Every object we surround ourselves with carries a story, and together they paint a picture of who we are and what truly matters to us. By choosing pre-loved over new, we can create a home that reflects not just our tastes, but our values in the world.

I could not have written this book without the many generous people who so trustingly opened their homes to me and my camera. A huge thank you to Esben Cordius; Christian Nørgaard; Niklas Søgaard and Martha Menko; Anders and Nina Lund Forup; Josias Juliussen; Anne Thorlund; Katrine Blinkenberg; Jesper Finderup and Stine Gosvig; Inger Grubbe; Trine Frausing; Laura Lange; Line Hallberg; Nina Marxen; Cecilie Bøllingtoft; Kristine Bendtsen; Peter Andersen and Karin Winther; Karen Schmidt; Cathrine Boye; Elias Hjorth Ingstrup; Camilla Brændgaard, and Nadia Chafra for allowing me to capture your beautiful homes and steal some of your best tips. Special thanks also to the shops Fil De Fer and Bbbigum for allowing me to take photos in your inspiring spaces.

Thank you as well to all the friends, colleagues and family members who have cheered me on along the way – and, most of all, to my wonderful partner, Rune, who has been extraordinarily patient, supportive and caring throughout the entire process. Thank you for solving my computer troubles, driving me to the farthest corners of the country, and taking care of dinner and household chores on all those evenings when I was hunched over my laptop. And thank you for always having faith in me, even when I didn't have faith in myself.

Finally, a massive thank you to everyone who has been kind enough to buy a copy of *The Vintage Way*. You have no idea how much your support means to me. I hope this book encourages you to explore vintage in your own way – whether that means rethinking how you decorate, being more intentional about what you bring into your home, or simply appreciating the beauty of things with a past.

Resources

Instagram-based Vintage Stores

✖

Denmark
@eliaselias
@danskform
@bbbigum
@baglommen
@rare__atelier
@ororoa_modern_design
@blameitonbacke
@galeriemodo
@14furniture

Rest of world
@modernisten
@studioschalling
@homeunion
@bohomeinteriors
@galerieprovenance
@counter.space
@pushpull.store
@enebyhome
@envanrijn
@galerienorthfield
@eesomeshop
@_modern_room
@keptlondon

Web-based Vintage Stores

✖

1st Dibs
www.1stdibs.com

Vinterior
www.vinterior.co

Chairish
www.chairish.com

Pamono
www.pamono.eu

Whoppah
www.whoppah.com

Etsy
www.etsy.com

Ebay
www.ebay.com

Auction Platforms for Vintage

✖

Auctionet
www.auctionet.com

LiveAuctioneers
www.liveauctioneers.com

Catawiki
www.catawiki.com

Index

✕

Danish-born Sarah Marie Winther is a freelance journalist and photographer, with a passion for hunting down vintage treasures. Based in Copenhagen, Sarah worked as the editor of the interiors section of the Danish national newspaper *Jyllands-Posten*, and is currently the content/social media manager at House of Finn Juhl, a Danish furniture company dedicated to preserving and continuing the legacy of designer Finn Juhl since 2001. *The Vintage Way* is her first book.

✕

First published in Great Britain in 2025 by Mitchell Beazley, an imprint of Octopus Publishing Group Ltd
Carmelite House
50 Victoria Embankment
London EC4Y 0DZ
www.octopusbooks.co.uk

An Hachette UK Company
www.hachette.co.uk

The authorized representative in the EEA is Hachette Ireland, 8 Castlecourt Centre, Dublin 15, D15 XTP3, Ireland (email: info@hbgi.ie)

Copyright © Sarah Marie Winther 2025

Distributed in the US by Hachette Book Group, 1290 Avenue of the Americas, 4th and 5th Floors, New York, NY 10104

Distributed in Canada by Canadian Manda Group, 664 Annette St., Toronto, Ontario, Canada M6S 2C8

ISBN 978 1 78472 973 8

A CIP catalogue record for this book is available from the British Library.

Printed and bound in China.

10 9 8 7 6 5 4 3 2 1

Publishing Director: Alison Starling
Creative Director: Jonathan Christie
Senior Managing Editor: Sybella Stephens
Copy Editor: Helen Ridge
Senior Production Manager: Katherine Hockley

FSC
MIX
Paper | Supporting responsible forestry
FSC® C008047
www.fsc.org

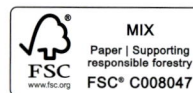